"This book proves that collective production of theological knowledge is not only possible but transformative. Challenging themes like sexuality, sexual health and rights, gender-based violence, and living with HIV are taken on with grace and care. . . . Through stories, process sharing, and theological reflection, the reader will discover that methodology matters—that theology can promote spiritually and socially liberating experiences, hope, and justice."

—MARCIA BLASI, Program Executive, Gender Justice and Women's Empowerment, Lutheran World Federation

"This collection of articles enhances the discussion on sexuality, corporality, and gender roles among faith actors and communities. The articles deliver profound theological knowledge and are committed to the transformation of oppression and injustice based on gender stereotypes. . . . I recommend this book to be used as a resource to guide faith-based communities, leaders, and actors in the treatment of themes still often considered taboo in religious contexts."

—ELAINE NEUENFELDT, Gender Program Manager, ACT Alliance

"For centuries, issues of gender and sexuality have raised violent reactions from people in power, notably churchmen. In these times, however, the ideologically tagged 'gender ideology' has become a weapon for violence against feminists and other champions of gender inclusion on the lips (screens) of whoever feels threatened by equality. This book offers insights not only on the issues . . . but on how we can come together for the sake of those who need a liberating theological word."

—MERCEDES L. GARCÍA BACHMANN, Director, Institute for Contextual Pastoral Studies, United Evangelical Lutheran Church, Argentina and Uruguay

Theology and Sexuality, Reproductive Health, and Rights

CHURCH OF SWEDEN RESEARCH SERIES

§

The Church of Sweden Research Series promotes research investigating the intersections of church, academy, and society. Its focus is on theology that is in lively conversation with the pressing issues of the world today, both from an academic and from an ecclesial perspective. What is the role of the churches in ever changing ecological, political, cultural, social and religious contexts? How is Christian teaching and practice affected by these changing currents? And how is the Lutheran tradition evolving amid such challenges? Through monographs and anthologies, the series makes available Swedish and Scandinavian scholarship in the English-speaking world, but also mirrors the worldwide connections of the Church of Sweden as part of its own identity.

General editor of the series (since 2020): Michael Nausner

Theology and Sexuality, Reproductive Health, and Rights

*Latin American Experiences
in Participatory Action Research*

Edited by
ANDRÉ S. MUSSKOPF
EDITH GONZÁLEZ BERNAL
MAURÍCIO RINCÓN ANDRADE

PICKWICK *Publications* · Eugene, Oregon

THEOLOGY AND SEXUALITY, REPRODUCTIVE HEALTH, AND RIGHTS
Latin American Experiences in Participatory Action Research

Church of Sweden Research Series 20

Pickwick Publications
An Imprint of Wipf and Stock Publishers
199 W. 8th Ave., Suite 3
Eugene, OR 97401

www.wipfandstock.com

PAPERBACK ISBN: 978-1-7252-7390-0
HARDCOVER ISBN: 978-1-7252-7391-7
EBOOK ISBN: 978-1-7252-7392-4

Cataloguing-in-Publication data:

Names: Musskopf, André S., editor. | González Bernal, Edith, editor. | Rincón Andrade,
Maurício, editor.

Title: Theology and sexuality, reproductive health, and rights : Latin American experiences in participatory action research / edited by André S. Musskopf, Edith González
Bernal and Maurício Rincón.

Description: Eugene, OR: Pickwick Publications, 2022 | Series: Church of Sweden Re-
search Series | Includes bibliographical references.

Identifiers: ISBN 978-1-7252-7390-0 (paperback) | ISBN 978-1-7252-7391-7 (hardcover) |
ISBN 978-1-7252-7392-4 (ebook)

Subjects: LCSH: Religion and sociology—Latin America. | Action research—Latin
America | Sex—Religious aspects—Christianity. | Human reproductive technology—
Religious aspects—Christianity.

Classification: BT708 T546 2022 (print) | BT708 (ebook)

This edition is based on a Spanish and a Portuguese original: Mauricio Rincón Andrade
and André S. Musskopf, editores. Teología y sexualidad, salud reproductiva y derechos:
experiencias desde la investigación acción participativa. Bogotá D.C., 2018. - André S.
Musskopf, Edith González Bernal, organição. Teologia e sexualidade, saúde reprodutiva e
direitos: Experiências em pesquisa participante. São Leopoldo 2018.

In memory of Remí Klein
(1952–2020)

Contents

About the Translation

WE ARE VERY GRATEFUL that the translation of this Latin American volume now is complete and available for an English-speaking public. We think that the global development in the context of the COVID-19 pandemic and related issues of sexual violence and discrimination are signs of the continued timeliness of this publication. We thank the Unit for Research and Analysis of the Church of Sweden for the financial support. And we would also like to thank Editage (www.editage.com) for the initial translation and English language editing. The remaining work was a transatlantic cooperative effort of three colleagues:

Jonas Ideström (Stockholm University College)

André S. Musskopf (Universidade Federal de Juiz de Fora)

Michael Nausner (Church of Sweden, Unit for Research and Analysis)

Contributors

Maurício Rincón Andrade, Professor and investigator at Facultad de Teología de la Pontificia Universidad Javeriana, Bógota, Colombia

Edith González Bernal, teaches at Facultad de Teología de la Pontificia Universidad Javeriana, Bógota, Colombia

Ezequiel Hanke, PhD in Systematic Theology

Ana L. D. S. Julio, PhD in Psychology, works for the Department of Justice and Citizenship of the State of Santa Catarina, Brazil.

Remí Klein, Professor at Faculdades EST, São Leopoldo, Brazil (deceased 2020)

Rebeca Lahass, Master student at Faculdades EST, São Leopoldo, Brazil

Edgar Antonio López, Professor of Theology at Facultad de Teología de la Pontificia Universidad Javeriana, Bógota, Colombia

André S. Musskopf, Professor of Religious Studies at Universidade Federal de Juiz de Fora, Brazil

Sandra Villalobos Nájera, post-doc Researcher at the National Autonomous University of Mexico

Sabrina Senger, Master in Theology, Project Assistant at the Gender and Religion Program at Faculdades EST, São Leopoldo, Brazil

Luciana Steffen, PhD in Practical Theology at Faculdades EST, São Leopoldo, Brazil

Presentation[1]

IT IS WITH GREAT joy that we present this book as the final document of the project titled Theology and Sexuality, Reproductive Health, and Rights. This project was carried out by the Faculdades EST headquartered in São Leopoldo, Brazil, and at the Pontificia Universidad Javeriana, based in Bogotá, Colombia. Civil-society organizations that work on issues related to the project were selected to participate through these institutions, including Fundación Huellas de Arte, Bogotá, Colombia; the patient group at the San Ignacio Hospital, Bogotá, Colombia; Coletivo Feminino Plural, Porto Alegre, Brazil; Fundação Luterana de Diaconia, Porto Alegre, Brazil; and the women's group of the Comunidade Luterana Floresta Imperial, Novo Hamburgo, Brazil.

This project relied on the valuable background of a previous five-year project, in which 26 Latin American theological studies institutions were trained in theology, with a thesis on theology and HIV/AIDS (Phase I, 2009–2013). This background made it possible for the research institutions to organize theological research groups during the 2014–2016 project with the participation of the teachers from Phase I, and even with experienced master's students. This background facilitated theological research and pastoral development in issues of sexuality and reproductive health and rights, in dialogue with community-based and faith-based organizations (grassroots groups, social movements, churches, ministers, pastoral agents, and civil society actors). It promotes and applies methodologies for Latin American popular education and participatory action research (PAR).

1. Most of this presentation is taken from the project's final report, written by Gustavo Driau, the general coordinator of the project in Latin America.

1

Context of the Project

In Latin America, in recent decades, the sociocultural approach to gender and sexual and reproductive health and rights has developed, and an extension of rights has been achieved through the continued struggles of multiple actors in civil society and the different sectors of governments. However, sexuality, health, discrimination, and stigma are not just matters of legislation. Sexuality, health, and religion have influenced each other throughout human experience, and this is also the case in Latin America.

Centuries of political, social, cultural, and religious oppression have prevented groups that are discriminated against because of their sexuality and gender from having access to equal rights and better living conditions. The predominant religious input rejects the empowerment of such people because of their identities, bodies, and overall health, and in a condemning manner, associates sexuality with sin. In Latin America, the violation of sexual and reproductive health rights has common roots in poverty, gender inequality, stigma, and prevailing cultural and religious norms.

People affected by issues of sexuality, reproductive health, and rights, receive messages of reprobation and condemnation from most churches, denying their dignity and their fundamental and equal human rights. These messages of reprobation and condemnation are based on an equivocal theological and pastoral reading, to whose revision and transformation this project has contributed.

People affected by issues of sexuality and sexual health that seek God (the experience of the sacred and the transcendent) should find in churches, healing and welcoming pastors who show the mercy and love of God. In recent decades, however, Latin America has also developed liberating theological approaches that, based on theologies of liberation, find a theological place (or locus as the place of encounter with the transcendent) in oppressed, denied, and discriminated persons. Among them are people living with HIV/AIDS (PLWHA), women, youth, sex workers, people with drug addictions, and sexual and gender minorities who are denied dignity, rights, and citizenship.

In this context, this project has contributed to highlighting liberating theological perspectives and religious thinking in relation to issues of sexuality and reproductive health and rights. To this end, the project supported the formation of church leadership (theologians, ministers, pastoral agents, and laity) capable of elaborating and making known an integral and liberating view of the bonds between the church and people affected by issues of sexuality and sexual and reproductive health. In this way, the project undoubtedly helped to alleviate religious prejudices and discrimination against minorities in relation to sexuality and reproductive health and rights.

The countries in which this project was developed (Brazil and Colombia) have relatively stable democratic regimes, which are making efforts to solve the deep historical problems of the founding stages of their states. The peace processes in Colombia and the fight against poverty in Brazil imply processes of structural change that are worth considering and supporting. When the project closed (2016), in both Colombia and Brazil, the societies experienced social and political upheavals that highlighted the fragility of these processes of change. The referendum that stalled peace processes in Colombia and the impeachment of President Dilma Rouseff in Brazil were clear evidence of how much work is still needed to consolidate progressive, democratic, and institutional changes in the region. In both cases, the predominant public voice of the religious sectors rejected progressive change and inclusive transformations.

Theory of Change Applied by the Project

The theory of change in the project aimed to transform the educational institutes connected to sexuality and reproductive health and rights (SRHR) and theology. It also aimed at influencing the studies and formation of new religious leaders, which in turn will influence the concepts and social prejudices connected to these issues.

Vision

The imagined change has been motivated by the vision of healthier and more inclusive relationships of academic theology to women, sexual minorities, and PLWHA, and those who suffer exclusion due to their gender. The aim is to strengthen contextual liberating theological approaches that confront and resist theological perspectives that deny rights. At the same time, it promotes an approach to ecumenical collaboration that seeks to strengthen the role of churches and faith-based organizations as agents of change in their communities and society.

Transformations

The strategy involved theologians and academic researchers of theology in a complementary relationship of mutual inquiry with grassroots groups that have vital and problematic lived experiences derived from sexuality, health, and rights. In addition, from that relationship, the question about the nature of the experience of God or the experience of the sacred that researchers and participating groups perceived was explored by sharing stories and life experiences.

The activities and testimonies of the participants throughout the project revealed that the institutions that produced theology collectively with people who have undergone liberating transformation through encounters with harmed peoples (through participatory action research methodologies) made notable contributions in favor of including, respecting, and dignifying oppressed people. In answering questions about the experience of God in vital and problematic moments, the project transformed the stigmas, exclusions, and invisibility of sexual minorities and PLWHA of the members of the participating populations and the researchers and theologians. This created an inclusive relationship of acceptance and collaboration.

Transformation on the Personal Level

The three-year project had a strong impact, as both academics and people from the participating populations identified shifts in their relationships and behaviors; for example, they recognized their initial limitations in understanding the "Other," who is different.

For academics, the Other (the different and unknown) entails people from grassroots groups with their own identities, illnesses, goals, and sufferings; it represents those who had never been in an academic research relationship. For the people from the participating populations, the Other is theologians with religious views and experiences (seen as a generic collective) of those subject to condemnation and stigma, and who now called upon them to collaborate on an equal level.

The people in both groups managed to make explicit changes in their mental models, recognizing that their compressed universe (mental map) was extended and enriched through their experience of the project and PAR. The invisibility and denial of the Other that they initially perceived in themselves had changed and become a more balanced and inclusive perception, recognizing the Other's differences and dignity.

4

These personal changes included increased self-esteem and respect for people in the participating populations. Through inclusive theological reflection, they shared a heightened sense of dignity. The academics acknowledged having experienced a radical change in their way of theologizing. For the grassroots groups, it was also significant to understand that they had a knowledge of life that the academics valued. In this horizontal relationship, everyone learned together at the same time.

Transformation in Relationships

The project facilitated multi-actor meeting spaces that encouraged dialogue and exchange of the participants' life experiences. These meeting spaces entailed a new definition of the relationship between academics and grassroots actors, between theologians and people who struggle to sustain their lives in the context of discrimination and exclusion.

The PAR enriched relationships of learning and teaching and made them horizontal. It also opened the space for a livelier and more complex epistemology. In this regard, the project definitively flattened and humanized the relationships between the researchers and participants.

Transformation of Cultural Models

The project focused mainly on changing the concrete and tangible perceptions of academic theologians toward PLWHA, feminist groups, hospital patients, and Christian educators who question the nature of the representations of sex and gender in their teachings. This transformation of cultural models was evident in the celebration of the International Meeting on Theology and Sexual Health and Rights in the main hall of Pontificia Universidad Javeriana at the end of 2016. Introducing this theme had significant implications and opened the doors and spaces for a transformation unthinkable eight years ago, when the relationship between the Church of Sweden and the Pontificia Universidad Javeriana began.

During the project and its development in the project countries (Colombia and Brazil), men and women experienced public debate and significant decision-making regarding sexual diversity and equal rights. In both countries, the Christian evangelical sectors have overtly opposed the diversity and equality of sexuality and rights. These public debates nonetheless reaffirmed the success of the applied theory of change, which obliges civil society and the state to improve public policies related to sexuality, reproductive health, and rights. In the process of policy making, it is necessary to have consistent contributions from contextual Liberation Theologies. In this sense, the project improved the capacity of theologians to make those contributions.

The project increased the capacity with which academic theology can work at the interface of churches (faith and the sacred) and civil society (the violated groups), to contribute to public policies related to sexuality and reproductive health and rights. The project clearly revealed the need for theology and churches with contextual and liberating theological approaches to accompany the struggle for equality, as well as the development of pastoral practices that do not punish and condemn but include and liberate.

Likewise, the spaces of more participatory monitoring produced, for the participants, experiential learning (instilled capacity). Due to the application of more transparent mechanisms of accountability for all actors, the project strengthened the ability of their faith-based organizations to empower groups and individuals socially in their human rights, clearly upholding basic principles of participation, non-discrimination, transparency, and accountability.

Synergies in the Church of Sweden

As a foreign donor for a project of this nature, the Church of Sweden had a double role. First, it fulfilled the function of a donor agency that established methods and routines for planning, monitoring, and evaluating the project. In this sense, the project has been an example of effective coordination, administration, transparency, and monitoring. The Church of Sweden provided invaluable cooperation with Gustavo Driau, an Argentine consultant who offered his services through the United Lutheran Church of Argentina and Uruguay. Driau's work was not limited to following up on the project but also facilitating working networks between the Faculdades EST and Pontificia Universidad Javeriana, to record the transformation in the project's participants and to synthesize mutual learning. His pastoral and simultaneous analytical perspective was invaluable for the effective functioning of the project. The Church of Sweden expresses its greatest gratitude to Gustavo Driau.

Second, the Church of Sweden is not a cooperation agency but a church, as its name implies. This body has conducted a project of sufficiently high quality to bring academia and civil society together to conduct theology on issues as controversial as sexual and reproductive health and rights. This approach opens the doors to theological reflection for the global South in a Nordic context. The PAR methods used in this project, which emphasize researchers as co-authors, involved the challenge of re-thinking the methods used by the Swedish researchers. Thus, the Church of Sweden illustrated the enormous potential for methodological, theoretical, and theological learning. The learning potential was evident in the clos-ing event, the International Meeting on Theology and Sexual Health and Rights, at the Pontificia Universidad Javeriana at the end of 2016. Several people from the Church of Sweden participated. This potential for mutual learning has barely been realized, so it must be developed through future activities.

Adriana Castellu Camp, Gustavo Driau, Verdiana Garcia
Coordinating Team of the Church of Sweden

Preface

HIV AND AIDS: STILL PLAGUING THE LAST AND LEAST

THE DOOM SO LONG associated with HIV and AIDS has been replaced in the northern hemisphere, and in the United States in particular, by modest optimism. While there is reason to celebrate the recent achievements of prophylactic measures, early diagnosis, and perhaps even the possibility of a vaccine to cure AIDS, not all people have access to these measures.[1] The virus still plagues millions of people around the globe. In the United States, HIV and AIDS continue to cause discrimination, as well as physical and emotional grief. The AIDS pandemic also allows us to map social trends and reveals taboos around human sexuality. The lives and deaths of people infected and affected by HIV and AIDS may not be important in the overall scheme of political or economic priorities, but they matter for those who are compassionate in love and bear witness to hope. Religious organizations and communities of faith are vitally needed to lift up those who are disenfranchised. This is the context and the call for theological engagement, to denounce injustice and promote wellbeing and abundance for all.

Stigma around HIV and AIDS

Ever since HIV/AIDS emerged as one of the most devastating viruses ever to affect humanity, its toll has been discrimination and death.[2] HIV and

---

1. See, for instance, how access to antiretroviral medication is connected to migration/immigration: https://www.theguardian.com/global-development/2019/feb/21/peru-sur vive-venezuelans-migrating-hiv-drugs?utm_term=RWRpdG9yaWFsXod1YXJkaWFuV G9kYXlVUyoxOTAyMjE%3D&utm_source=esp&utm_medium=Email&utm_campaig n=GuardianTodayUS&CMP=GTUS_email.

2. For a timeline of the dissemination for the virus, see https://www.avert.org/

AIDS have always carried stigma. When HIV (*Human Immunodeficiency Virus*) was first identified in the United States in the early 1980s, it was often labeled a gay illness (for instance, it was called "gay compromise syndrome"). However, realizing that the virus was not solely affecting the gay community, the US Centers for Disease Control and Prevention (CDC) officially established the name AIDS (Acquired Immune Deficiency Syndrome) in 1982.[3] The next year, the CDC announced four major groups at risk for AIDS in the United States, commonly referred to as the "Four-H Club:" homosexuals, hemophiliacs, heroin-users, and Haitians.

Paul Farmer's work in Haiti was instrumental in pointing out the stigmatizing effect on the Four-H Club.[4] Even though many individuals from these four communities were not at risk for AIDS, intense paranoia brought about by the lack of information and fear led to tremendous discrimination. AIDS was still a mysterious disease and contact with suspected carriers was regarded as dangerous. The CDC's warning may have done more harm than good. The Four-H group was heavily discriminated against, and AIDS became shrouded in shame and silence.

Eventually the panic created by HIV and AIDS in the 1980s gave way to greater understanding about conditions for transmission, forms of prevention, and accessibility to treatment. Knowing that the virus would not be contracted through sweat, tears, saliva, feces, or urine reduced the paranoia. However, the knowledge that it could be contracted through sexual intercourse, intravenous drug use, accidental blood exposure, and transmission from mother-to-child still carried a heavy stigma and the perception of possibly immoral practices. Instead of compassion and advocacy, many people's first reaction was to ask the lingering question: How did somebody contract the virus?

The answer to that question allocated less or more sympathy for an HIV-positive individual. Sexual contact and drug use were judged as moral lapses, while contamination through blood transfusion and vertical transmission (mother-to-child) were lamented as tragedies. To this day, HIV and AIDS come with social and emotional weight. People do not feel comfortable talking about it as they would about diabetes or cancer, for

---

professionals/history-hiv-AIDS/origin. The essay maps the trajectory of the HIV virus from crossing from chimps to humans in the 1920s (in what is now the Democratic Republic of Congo), the subtype of strain that made its way to Haiti, and its proliferation among with gay men in the United States, in the 1980s.

3. https://www.cdc.gov/mmwr/preview/mmwrhtml/00001163.htm.

4. Farmer, *AIDS and Accusation*.

instance. AIDS is a disease subject to judgment: one is guilty until proven innocent. But what if one's only "guilt" is to be born in poverty, with black or brown skin, or to be gender nonconforming?

HIV and AIDS are theological topics because they affect those who are vulnerable in our midst. Across the globe, individuals and communities affected or infected by the virus require spiritual and material support.

State of (Viral) Affairs

HIV (*human immunodeficiency virus*) has been one of the most devastating viruses to affect humanity. In the early days of the pandemic, a diagnosis of HIV was nearly always a death sentence. That situation has changed based on improved understanding about the virus and its effect on the immune system. AIDS (*acquired immunodeficiency syndrome)* is the stage of HIV infection wherein a person's immune system is fully compromised, leaving the body open to a wide range of potentially deadly diseases.

The main concern, after an HIV positive diagnosis, is to prevent the collapse of the immune system, a condition that would leave the body open to infections. After the initial (usually acute) infection, the HIV virus replicates silently, often without any sign of infection. Once the HIV virus has infected the body's immune system to the point of severely compromising it, the diagnosis becomes AIDS.[5] Some of the current research focuses on HIV's period of latency, when the virus continues to replicate silently. There has been some success in drawing the virus out of a latent stage (in which it can lie undetected for long periods) so that it can be destroyed.[6]

The deaths of more than 30 million people worldwide have been attributed to HIV since it was identified in 1981. Globally, there are approximately 36.9 million people living with HIV today, 69 percent of whom are in sub-Saharan Africa. According to the latest report of UNAIDS (The Joint United Nations Program on HIV and AIDS), an estimated 1.8 million individuals worldwide became infected with HIV in 2017—about 5,000 new infections per day. In the United States, approximately 1.2 million people

---

5. Technically, AIDS is defined by either a CD4 count of under 200 cells per microliter (μL) or by the diagnosis of a so-called AIDS-defining illness. Normal CD4 counts range on average from between 800 to 1600 cells per μL. Source: https://www.verywell-health.com/what-is-hiv-AIDS-48621.

6. See:https://www.theguardian.com/world/2018/nov/30/cure-for-hiv-world-AIDS-day.

are infected with HIV, according to the CDC. Of these, 20-25 percent are estimated to be undiagnosed.[7]

The World Health Organization (WHO) and the United Nations (through UNAIDS) have sought to reverse the trend through an initiative titled "90-90-90." The target is to implement national treatment programs by identifying 90 percent of people living with HIV through expanded testing, placing 90 percent of those confirmed on antiretroviral therapy, and ensuring that 90 percent of those on therapy are able to achieve complete viral suppression.[8]

Early diagnosis and access to antiretroviral therapy (ART) have helped to ameliorate the situation by improving the quality of life and lowering mortality of HIV-positive individuals. For instance, if untreated the average survival time for a person with AIDS is between six and 19 months. By contrast, a 35-year-old started on antiretroviral therapy (ART) can achieve a life expectancy equal to that of the general population.[9]

Among other improvements is the fact that an infected person today may take one pill daily, while at one time a cocktail of 30 pills was required. Today people who are infected will remain so for the rest of their lives, but scientists are beginning to ask if the biggest breakthrough—an out-and-out cure for tens of millions—could be in sight.

Medicating without Comprehensive Sexual Education

In 2012, the U.S. Food and Drug Administration (FDA) approved the drug Truvada as "pre-exposure prophylaxis" (PrEP) for use in HIV prevention.[10] WithPrEP, people at very high risk for HIV take a daily combination of two HIV medicines (tenofovir and emtricitabine) to lower their chances of infection. PrEP can stop HIV from taking hold and spreading through the body. If used as prescribed, PrEP reduces the risk of contracting HIV through sexual intercourse by more than 90 percent. Among people who inject drugs, it reduces the risk by more than 70 percent. The risk of getting HIV from sex can be even lower if PrEP is combined with condoms and other prevention methods.

7. See: https://www.hiv.gov/hiv-basics/overview/data-and-trends/global-statistics.

8. See: https://www.verywellhealth.com/united-nations-90-90-90-strategy-aims-to-end-hiv-epidemic-4105202.

9. See: https://www.verywellhealth.com/what-is-hiv-AIDS-48621.

10. The information about Pre Exposure Prophylaxis (PrEP) can found with the Center for Disease Control: https://www.cdc.gov/hiv/basics/prep.html.

Optimism is warranted: "When HIV-negative men who have sex with men (MSM) take PrEP daily, as prescribed, they lower their risk of contracting the virus by an estimated 99 percent or more."[11] The problem is in the operative words "as prescribed." Among men who have sex with men, "pre-exposure prophylaxis" has apparently led to a fall in condom use and an increase in other sexually transmitted infections (STIs).[12] This behavioral change is fueling questions about the correlation between the ever-growing number of people who take PrEP and their potential of contracting chlamydia, gonorrhea, syphilis or, in rarer cases, hepatitis C.

This trend is driven by multiple factors ranging from diminishing anxiety about HIV to the approval of effective treatments. What is clear is that the whole area of sexual education needs to be addressed. Currently, there is no standard curriculum for sexual education in schools, leaving young adults at the mercy of unreliable sources of information (gathered from friends or the internet). The topic of sexual education itself is contentious. Conversations in schools about human sexuality are often geared toward scaring young people away from engaging in sex and making it taboo, rather than providing honest dialogue and access to accurate information.

Religious organizations and faith communities have an opportunity to address human sexuality in a healthy, age-appropriate, and respectful manner. One such initiative is *Our Whole Lives* (OWL), a comprehensive curriculum for grades K-1 to adulthood.[13] It is important that human sexuality be understood not solely from a physiological perspective but factoring in body image, gender roles, emotions, peer pressures and harassment, caring, and self-respect and self-esteem. OWL has received accolades for

11. See: https://www.theguardian.com/society/2018/oct/21/truvada-prep-hiv-pre vention-sti-msm?utm_source=esp&utm_medium=Email&utm_ campaign=GU+Today+USA+-+Collections+2017&utm_term=288181&subid=854883 6&CMP=GT_US_collection.

12. See: https://www.ncbi.nlm.nih.gov/pubmed/29509889. "Pre-exposure prophy-laxis use was associated with a significant increase in rectal chlamydia (odds ratio [OR], 1.59; 95% confidence interval [CI], 1.19-2.13) and an increase in any STI diagnosis (OR, 1.24; 95% CI, .99-1.54). The association of PrEP use with STI diagnoses was stronger in later studies. Most studies showed evidence of an increase in sex without a condom among PrEP users."

13. See: https://www.uua.org/re/owl. OWL was developed by the Unitarian Univer-salist Association and the United Church of Christ in 1999. There are six OWL curricula: grades K-1, 4–6, 7–9, 10–12, young adult, and adult. Facilitators may use the supple-mental *Sexuality and Our Faith* publication when teaching in an exclusively UU or UCC context. Other faith traditions can choose to use and adapt the supplement. All other permutations of OWL may draw only from the secular OWL curricula.

its holistic approach that emphasizes safe and supportive peer groups and acceptance of diversity. It has a social justice approach to inclusive sexual education. An example of this holistic approach is parent orientation, affirming parents as their children's primary sexuality educators.

Healthy and honest information about human sexuality "dismantles stereotypes and assumptions, builds self-acceptance and self-esteem, fosters healthy relationships, improves decision making, and has the potential to save lives."[14] While medication is absolutely necessary, it is equally necessary to engage in a comprehensive and robust conversation about human sexuality and its interface with other aspects of human life. Faith communities and their members can be partners in this conversation, celebrating human sexuality as part of God's good creation, while inviting further reflection on the conditions and predicaments that prevent human life from flourishing.

Intersectionality between Race, Gender, Age, and Class

Not all treatment for HIV and AIDS is equally accessible to everyone. In the United States, HIV rates are higher in African American communities. The disparity is such that, despite representing only 12 percent of the U.S. population, African Americans account for 48 percent of all new HIV infections.[15] Culture or sexual behavior cannot explain away these numbers. Instead, the HIV epidemic offers a snapshot of social and economic disparities. HIV and AIDS serve as an intersectional lens that reveals deep-seated and institutional inequalities, affected by socio-economic factors, such as poverty, lack of access to quality healthcare, stigma, and disproportionately high rates of arrest and incarceration.

The U.S. CDC released a first-of-its-kind report assessing the lifetime risk of HIV, by state and by key at-risk populations.[16] Although HIV is still a stigmatizing condition, the report shows that education, awareness campaigns, and the latest medical breakthroughs have helped prevention and treatment. What is not happening, however, is equal access to these resources. People who live in the south of the country (the region with the highest rate of new HIV infections) are at the greatest risk. One particular group—gay black men—was reported to have a startling one-in-two

14. See: https://www.uua.org/re/owl.

15. See: https://www.verywellhealth.com/why-hiv-rates-are-high-in-african-ameri-can-communities-4151837.

16. See: https://www.cdc.gov/hiv/library/reports/hiv-surveillance.html.

chance of contracting HIV in a lifetime, irrespective of age or geographic location.[17] It is estimated that 50 percent of African American gay men will contract HIV, precisely due to intersecting vulnerabilities.[18]

> In the US, the situation divides depending on geography, and, most strikingly, race. According to the Centers for Disease Control, African Americans accounted for 44% of HIV diagnoses in 2016, despite comprising only 12% of the population. And the disproportion seems to be growing. That year, HIV diagnoses among African American gay and bisexual men aged 25 to 34 increased 30%. If you are a young gay black man in America, you have a one in two chance of contracting the virus—compared with a one in 11 chance if you are a white gay man.[19]

There are interlocking factors leading to the disproportionate effect of HIV in the deep south; most are related to pervasive stigma related to HIV, poverty, racial inequality, and bias.[20] There are also funding inequalities. In 2014, the Deep South received $35 per HIV-affected person in private grants, while the U.S. average was $116.[21] As the manifestation of HIV decreased in the white population, it also dwindled from public consciousness. Many non-profit organizations that had originally been created to combat HIV and AIDS changed their focus, turning their attention to equal marriage rights instead. While a white gay man has a one in 11 chance of becoming HIV positive, for an African American gay man there is a 50-50 risk (one in two).

> For men who grow up gay in the south, this kind of shame and stigma makes them less likely to seek information about, and protection for, their sex lives. Closeted sex is inherently dangerous, because it happens in places where it is not safe to talk openly to

17. See: https://www.theguardian.com/world/2018/jun/01/silent-epidemic-black -gay-men-in-us-face-50-50-risk-of-hiv.

18. See: https://www.verywellhealth.com/why-50-of-gay-black-men-will-get-hiv-3 896687.

19. See: https://www.theguardian.com/commentisfree/2018/may/30/the-guardian -view-on-hiv-in-the-us-an-invisible-epidemic.

20. "Factors that have been identified as contributors to the disproportionate effects of HIV in the Deep South include pervasive HIV-related stigma, poverty, higher levels of sexually transmitted infections, racial inequality and bias, and laws that further HIV-related stigma and fear." For full analysis see https://www.ncbi.nlm.nih.gov/ pubmed/28247067.

21. See: https://www.theguardian.com/world/2018/jun/01/silent-epidemic-black -gay-men-in-us-face-50-50-risk-of-hiv.

people who may be able to help. What follows can be a lack of knowledge about safe sex or a huge underestimation of the risk of infection.[22]

While the black, gay, and bisexual male population has the highest risk of HIV infection in the United States, the population with the next highest risk is Latinos. A *machista*culture often prevents men from openly discussing their sexuality, especially if they are gender nonconforming. Thus, a particularly worrisome sign for this population is that infections are increasing among its young people—the country's youngest and largest minority group. According to the CDC, HIV infections and new HIV diagnoses have been decreasing nationally, but both are increasing among African Americans and Latinos.[23] This increase is largely among gay and bisexual men under the age of 30.

Health interventions, like PrEP (the HIV prevention drug), are not reaching these populations. Of PrEP users, nearly 70 percent are white, while Latinos comprise 13 percent and African Americans roughly 11 percent.[24] Access to health care, education, and a safe environment to talk about human sexuality is not a reality for everybody. To the contrary–toxic masculinity spreads its nefarious roots through gender constructs, vilifying any sexual practice that does not conform to heterosexuality.[25] The results can be catastrophic.

We cannot forget that people are suffering and dying because of HIV and AIDS, and that the most vulnerable population is particularly prone to its consequences. Communities of faith can be potent advocates. By pointing out overlapping vulnerabilities, theological reflection becomes contextual and honors the experiences of groups that might be disenfranchised.

22. See: https://www.theguardian.com/world/2018/jun/01/silent-epidemic-black-gay-men-in-us-face-50-50-risk-of-hiv.

23. See: https://www.cdc.gov/hiv/group/racialethnic/africanamericans/index.html.

24. "PrEP users for whom race/ethnicity data were available, 68.7% were white, 11.2% were African American or black (black), 13.1% were Hispanic, and 4.5% were Asian. Approximately 7% of the estimated 1.1 million persons who had indications for PrEP were prescribed PrEP in 2016, including 2.1% of women with PrEP indications (6). Although black men and women accounted for approximately 40% of persons with PrEP indications (6), this study found that nearly six times as many white men and women were prescribed PrEP as were black men and women." Source: https://www.cdc.gov/mmwr/volumes/67/wr/mm6741a3.htm?s_cid=mm6741a3_e&fbclid=IwAR3xUvqpWmLXBfzc34Ddfe4rM3ArxoClngDeDW8Am_fzn7OEWpzyL42P3pA.

25. See: https://www.theguardian.com/society/2019/feb/15/hiv-AIDS-us-young-latino-men-bronx-new-york.

It also validates the spiritual journeys, the laments, and cries for hope of those who are infected and affected by HIV and AIDS. The pandemic is also an invitation for faith communities to become more involved in local and national debates on access to healthcare, racism, sexism, and gender bias—among other urgent topics. HIV and AIDS can be reduced if there is the political will to do so. But the investment in technologies, education, and services for all is a matter of advocacy and social justice.

Faith communities are always looking for new ways to make the good news of hope and love meaningful in the here and now. This book shows us how the challenges regarding HIV and AIDS have been addressed in Latin America and the Caribbean. With the financial support of the Church of Sweden, two theological institutions—Faculdades EST, in Brazil, and Pontificia Universidad Javeriana, in Colombia—have developed research on human sexuality, reproductive rights, and the HIV and AIDS pandemic. The chapters of this book present a broad framework of theological reflection and practices of social inclusion. The contributors show how changes in attitude and mentality can lead to sexual practices that are safe and healthy. Through dialogue and openness, they compel us to overcome the bias and stigma that still surround HIV and AIDS.

In the United States, there is an ongoing need for advocacy on behalf of those who are most vulnerable. This includes those who do not have access to appropriate healthcare, education, and HIV and AIDS prevention. The theological reflections in this book present an invitation for a change of minds and hearts: high-minded moralizing, particularly from religious groups, might give way to empathy and acceptance if the stories of those who are bullied and stigmatized are heard. Comprehensive sexual education can help us replace the fear of STIs, by promoting an ethics of consent, reciprocity, and sensuality. The chapters of this book can aid us in envisioning human sexuality not as an expression of sin and a reason for guilt, as is often preached, but a celebration of the creative power of love. The HIV and AIDS pandemic is an ongoing call for people of faith to live in passion and compassion, aware and attentive to the last and least in our midst.

Wanda Deifelt

Bibliography

Farmer, Paul. *AIDS and Accusation: Haiti and the Geography of Blame.* Berkeley: University of California Press, 1992.

1

Introduction

LATIN AMERICA HAS EXPERIENCED abuse and violence. The colonial project that attacked the land, its peoples (especially women) and cultures is historically reinforced by fake independence events chanted in glorious and heroic hymns, military dictatorships that are from time to time praised as peace and order keeping, and capitalist neoliberal economic political agendas that are made irresistible through sophisticated and elaborate media advertisement and propaganda that makes all exploitation look *mainstream*. The "motherland" *(madre tierra)*, in the many meanings it takes on, is raped again and again through the extraction of natural sources (transformed into goods), the subjugation of workers through predatory employment practices, and the perpetuation of social relations based on discrimination, injustice, and inequality led by national and international elites.[1] But there has been and there continues to be resistance and struggle.

Decolonial studies and emancipatory practices have shown the intricate and persistent element of "coloniality" in Latin American societies, even in so-called post-colonial contexts. Even after epically described independence processes promised sovereignty and freedom from oppression, the overthrow of military dictatorship regimes by popular and revolutionary movements, the signing of internal and external peace agreements, the implementation of (re)democratization and elections (mostly representative and not really participatory), the region remains a conflict zone. Many interests are being played out—not for the wellbeing of the people, especially not for the most poor and vulnerable. Capitalism, racism, and

1. Cardoso-Pereira, "Dos filhos deste solo não sou mãe gentil."

19

patriarchy in the current colonial experiences color the realities of the continent, notwithstanding the plurality and diversity of countries, cultures, and historical processes throughout the region.[2] In recent events, gender and sexuality, articulated in religious discourse and practice, have once again shown how those issues are key to understanding and confronting matters of violence and oppression (at an individual and communal level, but also in broader political and economic processes).

Gender-based violence in Latin America is epidemic and well-documented, as is its relation to economic and religious discourses and practices. The same can be said about homophobic, lesbophobic, and transphobic violence (with the rising figures and cruelty around transfeminicides). There are several organizations, campaigns, initiatives, laws, and public policies that have, in different contexts, denounced and confronted this reality. The movement #NIUNAMENOS is one powerful example of such a cry for justice and an end to gender-based violence.[3] Although an Argentinian example, this campaign resonated throughout the Americas. "The movement that started in 2015 in Argentina and gathered millions, crossed the borders reaching several Latin-American countries such as Chile, Uruguay, Ecuador, etc., and every June 3rd, day of the death of Páez, the march is repeated and the struggle for the end of feminicide and for gender equality continues."[4]

Thirteen years earlier, also in Argentina, the "National campaign for the right to safe and free abortion" was created and, in 2018, had its most important win. That June, the House of Deputies approved the law that would allow for the interruption of pregnancy up to the 14th week.[5] The law was later rejected by the Senate, but the "green wave"[6] ran through all of Latin America and echoed in similar movements all over the continent.

---

2. Segato, *La crítica de la colonialidade em ocho ensayos.*

3. "In 2015, after a series of news about feminicides without resolution and, mainly, after the case of Chiara, a 14-year-old pregnant girl who was killed and buried in the backyard of her boyfriend, a big wave of revolt ran through Argentina. Under the hashtag #NiUnaMenos called by the journalist Marcela Ojeda, the movement got force and voice and culminated in the first public manifestation called for June 3rd 2015 in front of the Congress square in Argentina, with more than 200 thousand people." Gabardo and Lima-Lopes, "Ni una menos," 45.

4. Maciel and Silva Neto, "Resistência das mulheres latino-americanas."

5. Frayssinet, *Direito ao aborto.*

6. The main symbol of this movement was a green triangular scarf with the inscription "sexual education to decide, contraceptives not to abort, legal abortion not to die."

The #NIUNAMENOS movement certainly gave momentum and strength to this renewed movement for reproductive rights.[7]

It is no coincidence that in this same context a strong oppositional force emerged. After a heavy campaign to counteract any movement, reflection, academic study, public policy in favor of sexual and reproductive health and rights, the expression "gender ideology" became part of common and everyday conversations in Latin America.[8] With a very conflated and imprecise meaning, the term questioned the presence of sexual education, discussed diversity and equality in schools, and promoted political right-wing agendas in governments and electoral processes.[9] However, under the premise of defending "the family," groups sponsored and continue to sponsor attacks on anything related to gender. Such groups mix up religious discourses and practices (either because the group members themselves are identified as religious or because public figures that make use of and replicate this expression are somehow identified with religion—mostly Christian).

In Brazil, the "moral panic" around the so-called "gender ideology" resulted in removing the words "gender" and "diversity" from the National Education Plan, as well as many state and municipal plans.[10] The idea of a "gender ideology" also played a significant role in the 2018 electoral process, as it was used by several candidates and spread through the fake news disseminated through social media. The notion that "gender ideology" threatened families and the country was associated with left-wing candidates and governments (many times called "communists") and resulted in a wave of death threats that affected people in many ways.[11]

---

7. Dip, "Argentina."

8. Miskolci and Campana, "Ideologia de gênero," 725–47.

9. Junqueira, "Ideologia de gênero," 25–52.

10. Reis and Eggert, "Ideologia de gênero," 138.

11. Débora Diniz, an important researcher in the area of sexual and reproductive health and rights who presented at the Supreme Court Hearing on abortion in 2018 has since been living and exile and under the protection of international human rights organizations. Jean Wyllys, elected for his third term as Federal Deputy, announced in January 2019 that he would not take on office and would not return to Brazil because of fear for his and his family's life and the incapacity of the State to protect his rights. Soon after that Sabrina Bittencourt, known for her activism in defense of victims of sexual abuse by religious leaders, committed suicide while living in exile and under international human rights protection. Those are just a few examples of the most public events that show the current situation in Brazil.

In recent years, Colombia has had peace negotiations with the Revolutionary Armed Forces of Colombia (FARC). Those were meaningful moments for a society that, for more than 60 years, lived in armed conflict. The expectations of the peace process permeated all levels of social life. In schools and universities, it meant adopting language about reconciliation and peace. It is important to acknowledge how difficult the process of negotiation has been and how difficult it has been to implement the peace agreements made between the government and the demobilized guerrilla. The greatest challenge is to build new scenarios for peace and reconciliation for everyone. The current context has suggested the potential of imaginaries of peace and reconciliation, which are distant from the Colombian population. Nonetheless, those imaginaries are weak. The legacy of violence has been so strong that it has polarized the society. But, even so, the people are tired of the violence and are committed to forging a peaceful existence together. In this context, the "gender ideology" campaign also influenced the vote of people who said "no" to the peace agreement in 2016.[12]

This book does not specifically deal with those events or its consequences. The articles, in different ways, however, deal with the issues that lie at the heart of peaceful reconciliation and its challenges to theological research and knowledge. This book, thus, adds a twofold contribution to those debates. On the one hand, it offers valuable methodological insights, particularly putting in dialogue participatory and action research developed in the Latin American context and theological knowledge. Participatory and action research methods are valuable both for the debates on the relevance and impact of research practices and for the effective changes it can make in the daily struggles of groups and communities. On the other hand, it presents ways in which to engage theology, and more generally religion, in the public policy related discussions about sexual and reproductive health and rights both, at an academic and at a community level. Thus, the goals of the project resonate with the research behind this publication.

The project that named this publication—Theology and Sexuality, Reproductive Health and Rights—was developed from 2014 to 2016 by the Church of Sweden, Faculdades EST (Brazil), and Pontificia Universidad Javeriana/PUJ (Colombia). For three years, four research projects were developed involving diverse people, groups, and organizations. Several activities were designed with the goal of potentializing the research themes and exchanging knowledge and research practices.

12. Muelle, "Cómo hacer necro políticas."

The project was a continuation of a previous one—Theology and HIV/AIDS—developed from 2010 to 2012 in four theological institutions in Latin America. The focus of the first project was theological education at a master's level. The project also facilitated professors' meetings and international seminars that gathered professors, students, and religious leaders; that project resulted in the production of several bibliographical materials.[13]

The keys and challenges for the second phase of the project were defined in Costa Rica at the 2013 evaluation seminar of this first projectand were also based on an evaluation carried out by a specialized consultancy. The evaluations pointed out that it was necessary to continue research in this field, by looking at wider issues implicated in the HIV/AIDS epidemic that render individuals and social groups vulnerable to infection and unable to access treatment. Further, the evaluations called for closer reflections and actions developed in Latin America, particularly in the field of Liberation Theologies and the instruments of popular education and Participatory Research. So:

> The strategy of the project points to developing academic capacities at the theological institutions in Latin America such that positive changes emerge in the relationship between theology and themes of sexuality, reproductive health and rights; this includes developing pastoral capacities in the churches and faith-based organizations. [...] Phase II proposed that the institutions organize a group of theological research, in which people who earned a Master's Degree in Phase I (and other interested parties) could develop and participate in theological research and pastoral development activities around these themes, with community based and faith-based organizations (grassroots groups, social movements, churches, ministers, pastoral agents, and civil society actors), while applying and promoting Latin American popular education and participatory action-research methodologies.[14]

---

13. About the project, see Streck, *Teología y VIH*, xix–xxii. The book gathers articles written by students who were part of the project. An abbreviated version was also published in English: Streck, *Theology and HIV*. Another material produced was the dossier "Teologia e HIV e AIDS." The Project developed in Latin America followed a similar experience developed in Africa with the support of the Church of Sweden. See Ward and Leonard, *Theology of HIV and AIDS on Africa's East Coast*.

14. *Teología, Sexualidad, Salud Reproditiva*.

To accomplish these goals and to develop this proposal, the Church of Sweden called upon Faculdades EST and Pontificia Universidad Javeriana.Each institution chose two research projects to be carried out. Besides the activities directly connected to the research projects, other activities of exchange, formation, and partnership with groups and organizations were conducted.

The first "Exchange Seminar" with researchers from both institutions took place at Faculdades EST in 2014 and, in 2015, a second Seminar took place at Pontificia Universidad Javeriana. In 2015, a unified working group was set up with representatives of both institutionsto participate in the IV Latin American Congress on Gender and Religion, organized by the Gender and Religion Program and the Gender Research Group at Faculdades EST.[15] In 2016, professor exchange programs were accomplished[16] and also the International Meeting of Theology, Sexual Health, and Rights marked the closing of the Project, in Bogotá, Colombia.

As one of the results of this project, this book presents the final reports of the four research projects. The first two chapters present the results of the research developed at Faculdades EST, dealing specifically with a wider debate about epistemology and education around sexual and reproductive health and rights. This framework seeks to answer questions about processes of knowledge production and pedagogical action in the theological and religious field. The following chapters, which complete this publication, are a result of the research projects developed at Pontificia Universidad Javeriana. They have as a main theme the HIV and AIDS epidemic. They bring those experiences to the field of reflection of theology by addressing the epidemic in diverse ways, by working with specific groups and using participatory methodologies.

The first text, which presents the results of the research project coordinated by Dr. André S. Musskopf, focuses on the production of theological knowledge about and from discussions on sexual and reproductive health and rights. It describes the processes developed in the field research that interfere and contribute to its accomplishment. It presents the organizations and groups with which the team worked—Coletivo Feminino Plural,

---

15. As a result, a volume of the Journal *Coisas do Gênero* was organized with the theme of the project, gathering texts presented during the Congress at the Working Group. See *Coisas do Gênero.*

16. Dr. Olga Consuelo Vélez was at Faculdades EST for one week developing research activities and participating in local activities and, in the same way, Dr. André S. Musskopf was for one week at Pontificia Universidad Javeriana.

Fundação Luterana de Diaconia, and Grupo de Mulheres da Comunidade Floresta Imperial, the activities developed, and the lessons learned. It reflects on the production of knowledge experienced through participatory research and the systematization of experiences, as described by Oscar Jara, pointing to the possibility of new languages and formulations in the field of theology.

The research coordinated by Dr. Remí Klein is presented in the sequence focusing on Christian Education. It presents the results of document-based research about gender in education. First, it analyzes perspectives of Brazilian educational policies, particularly the Education Plans, and themes of gender and diversity in the pedagogical materials produced by the Evangelical Church of Lutheran Confession in Brazil (ECLCB) for children and teenagers. Using methodology proposed by Marie-Christine Josso and leaders in the field of Christian Education in the ECLCB, it further describes and investigates the work developed with a research formation group. They received a proposal to construct and discuss "writings of oneself" related to issues of gender and sexuality, as well as proposals for Christian Education about those themes in the Church.

Chapter 3 presents the results of the research accomplished by the Theology and Contemporary World Research Group, coordinated by Dr. Silvia Susana Becerra. The text deals with discussion about HIV/AIDS and spirituality from the work accomplished in partnership with the Infectious Diseases Unit of the University Hospital San Ignacio. It situates the context of the HIV and AIDS epidemic in Colombia, presents a methodological discussion about Investigación-Acción Participativa (IAP), and describes the activities carried out with hospital patients with HIV/AIDS. Activities included a survey with 123 patients seeking to identify elements their experiences, particularly regarding spirituality. In-depth interviews were carried out with a smaller group of patients (called Akasa). Thematic workshops about issues related to the research and art therapy were held. The use of life experiences narratives, field diaries, and focal groups was highlighted. These activities offer the material for the reflection that follows on spirituality, body and embodiment, sexuality and gender, opening pathways for continuous reflection and production on those themes.

The text that closes this publication presents a reflection about the biblical narrative of 2 Samuel 13:1–22 developed through the joint work between the Didaskalia Research Group, coordinated by Dr. José Luis Mesa Rueda, and Fundación Huellas de Arte, formed by women living with HIV and/or AIDS. The research was based on the contextual reading of the Bible and the *Investigación-Acción Participativa* (IAP). The article initially presents a discussion about those two methodological perspectives and the relationship between them, as it applies to the research. After a presentation of Fundación Huellas de Arte and its context, the text uses the tools and commentaries from the field of biblical research to present an analysis of the biblical text of 2 Samuel 13:1–22, which speaks about the sexual abuse suffered by Tamar. Finally, it systematizes the results of the exercise of contextual reading developed with the participants of the organization. It highlights the themes that emerged in the process of reading, interpreting, and offering new possibilities of re-reading that emerge from the concrete reality of the people involved in the process of interpretation.

This book is, no doubt, a great contribution for the theological field and pastoral practice, as well as for academic research and broader public. Its contribution becomes even more relevant in the current context in which issues related to gender and sexuality have taken center stage in political debates and government actions that tend to deny and violate human rights. The emergence of conservative and fundamentalist groups and their presence and impact in the public spaces and institutions in the recent history of Brazil and Colombia, as well as in the history of Latin America as a whole, cannot be underestimated. As shown in the first part of this introduction, it is possible to observe a dismantling of the democratic structures and public policies accomplished after great struggle.

The context in which this work was carried out allowed for the sharing of knowledge and experiences among the two institutions and made visible the possibility of dialogue and ecumenical work. It is important to highlight that in the Latin American context the social, political, religious, and educational processes of the last 10 years have sought to affirm human rights, i.e. a search for equality, respect for difference, the plurality of religious expressions, and the modification of patriarchal practices in the social and ecclesiastical movements. The initiatives of cooperation, such as the one we have been experiencing with the Church of Sweden and the two partner institutions, contribute significantly to processes of conversion. They change the mentality of fundamentalisms that are reproduced at individual and social levels. Such reproductions give rise to intolerance and violence toward difference—evidenced by violence against women. In the work done by the Church of Sweden, we highlight the gender equity efforts that promote the visibility of women's leadership. In addition, ecumenical dialogue is strengthened.

Sexuality, reproductive health, and rights are not only specific and localized themes, but they are also at the center of the organization of human relations. This is evident in the attacks and manipulations of religious discourse on those subjects, which fuel hatred, discrimination, and violence. That is why theological reflections constructed from liberating and participatory research practices, as presented in this book, are fundamental to reverse those trends. Religion itself is relevant in the construction of democratic processes that can point to a positive future on the continent and in the world.

André S. Musskopf, Edith González Bernal, Maurício Rincón Andrade

Bibliography

Cardoso-Pereira, Nancy. "Dos filhos deste solo não sou mãe gentil: do imaginário da mãe-terra à crítica eco-feminista." *Caminhos* 11 (2013) 123–38.

Coisas do gênero 1:2 (2015). http://periodicos.est.edu.br/index.php/genero/issue/view/279.

Díaz, Noelia Belen, and Alejandro Hernán López. "Ni una menos: el grito en común." Final paper, Universidad Nacional de la Plata—Facultad de Periodismo y Comunicación Social, 2016.

Dip, Andrea. "Argentina: do 'nenhuma a menos' à legalização do aborto." https://apublica.org/2018/07/argentina-do-nenhuma-a-menos-a-legalizacao-do-aborto/.

Estudos teológicos 52:2 (2012).

Frayssinet, Fabiana. "Direito ao aborto: a onda verde na américa latina." https://outraspalavras.net/feminismos/direito-ao-aborto-a-onda-verde-na-america-latina/.

Gabardo, Maristella and Rodrigo Esteves de Lima-Lopes. "Ni Una Menos: Ciência Das Redes E Análise De Um Coletivo Feminista." *Revista Humanidades e Inovação* 5 (2018) 44–58.

Junqueira, Rogério Diniz. "Ideologia de gênero': a gênese de uma categoria política reacionária—ou: a promoção dos direitos humanos se tornou uma 'ameaça à família natural?" In *Debates contemporâneos sobre Educação para a sexualidade*, edited by Paula Regina Costa Ribeiro and Joanalira Corpes Magalhães, 25–52. Rio Grande: Ed. da FURG, 2017.

Maciel, Thaynná Soares, and Antonio Carlos Batista da Silva Neto. "Resistência Das Mulheres Latino-Americanas: ni una menos." https://editorarealize.com.br/revistas/conages/trabalhos/TRABALHO_EV112_MD1_SA11_ID152_10052018134657.pdf.

Miskolci, Richard, and Maximiliano Campana. "Ideologia de gênero': notas para a genealogia de um pânico moral contemporâneo." *Revista Sociedade e Estado* 32 (2017) 725–47.

Muelle, Camila Esguerra. "Cómo hacer necropolíticas en casa: ideología de género y acuerdos de paz en Colombia." *Sexualidad, Salud y Sociedad–Revista Latinoamericana* 27 (2017) 172–98.

Reis, Toni, and Edla Eggert. "Ideologia de gênero: uma falácia construída sobre os planos de educação brasileiros." *Educação Social* 38 (2017) 9–26.

Segato, Rita. *La crítica de la colonialidade em ocho ensayos y uma antropología por demanda.* Buenos Aires: Prometeo, 2013.

Streck, Valburga S. "Introducción." In *Teología y VIH y Sida em América Latina*, edited by Valburga Streck, xix–xxii. São Leopoldo: Oikos, 2013.

Streck, Valburga, ed. *Theology and HIV and AIDS in Latin America.* São Leopoldo: Oikos, 2013.

"Teologia e HIV e AIDS." *Estudos teológicos* 52 (2012).

Teología, Sexualidad, Salud Reproditiva y Derechos. Document. Arquivo Reitoria.

Ward, Edwina, and Gary Leonard, eds. *A Theology of HIV and AIDS on Africa's East Coast.* Uppsala: Swedish Institute of Mission Research, 2008.

2

Producing Theological Knowledge on Sexuality with Religious Groups and Social Organizations[1]

André S. Musskopf, Luciana Steffen, Sabrina Senger, Rebeca Lahass, Sandra Villalobos Nájera, Ezequiel Hanke, Ana L. D. S. Julio

INTRODUCTION

The field of sexual and reproductive health and rights (SRHR), as a significant area of knowledge production and political activity, has been in focus recently, but not always for the noblest reasons. Nevertheless, the works of feminist, women's, and LGBT (lesbian, gay, bisexual, and transgender)[2] social movements in the production of academic knowledge and in public policies have been making progress in recent decades. This has been the case despite the questioning and interpositions that threaten achievements and increase the precariousness of the living conditions of people and social groups who have had their rights violated.

1. This research was funded by the Church of Sweden, through the *Theology and Sexuality, Reproductive Health, and Rights* project. It was also approved by the Universal Call of the National Council on Research and Technological Development (CNPq) and received a grant of BRL 6,000.00.

2. LGBT is an acronym that has been expanded in various ways in order to recognize the variety of gender-identity based cultures. See: https://en.wikipedia.org/wiki/LGBT.

Religious discourse and practice, in many cases, have fueled intense confrontations between antagonistic groups and claims of legitimacy that seek to define consolidation around SRHR. In addition, proposals and practices constructed in the religious field itself have not only affirmed the pertinence of reflecting and acting on these issues, but also offered alternatives to the well-worn religious positions that impede access to health and that limit the full exercise of SRHR. Thus, these arguments are also being put forward as a challenge within the field of theological research.

Theology, whether in the context of academic production or as a language of faith,[3] is a privileged field for this discussion. Not only has "religion" once again become one of the central themes of contemporary reality—if it ever stopped being one—but it is very close to people's most vital and liminal experiences. This gives rise to reflection on how the processes of meaning that are converted into knowledge come about in the first place. Further, it confronts how they are recognized, incorporated, marginalized, or forgotten. The same can be said about gender and sexuality. Feminist studies have demonstrated that "gender" is the first form of power inscription on bodies; queer studies have deepened this discussion by affirming the inseparable relationship between sexuality and power. Marcella Althaus-Reid, for example, asserted that all theology is "a sexual act."[4] In this way, the question about theological knowledge production *about* gender and sexuality is, at the same time, a question regarding theological knowledge, which is itself the *result* of an epistemology of gender and sexuality.[5]

In addressing these questions, we seek to demonstrate how they are involved in theact of research, which undoubtedly defined the paths taken in the development of this project, *Theology and Sexuality, Reproductive*

3. The term "experiences of faith" refers to the broader set of possible experiences that are not necessarily related to what is commonly understood as "religious." It refers to experiences that mark people's history, to the point of producing language to express these experiences, so that they become more or less permanent and present in their trajectories.

4. Althaus-Reid, *Indecent Theology*.

5. Musskopf (*Via(da)gens teológicas*) demonstrated how, in the Brazilian (and Latin American) context, the experience of religion and sexuality are affected by what has been called "ambiguity," in the way that each of these dimensions is lived separately and in how they blend into people's experience. Traditional theologies have masked this ambiguity and constructed systematic discourses that deny people's experience by constructing an ideal reality in which (in order to be considered "normal"), one must conform. That is why queer (or indecent) theology has the potential to reshape the field of theology.

Health, and Rights (TSRHR). In addition, we seek to highlight theoretical assumptions made in the research that generally and without pretension of purity, can be grouped into Liberation Theologies (Latin American, Feminist, and Queer), Liberation Pedagogies (Popular Education, Participant Research, and the Systematization of Experiences), and Feminist, Gender, and Queer Studies. These broad and diverse theoretical fields, in an independent or interconnected way, inform the research methodology. The present findings are, themselves, epistemology put into practice.

We do not seek to present, according to a modern, positivist, and scientific rationality, formulations that prove a given discovery, but to produce knowledge, insofar as one may speak of the production of knowledge as a circular and cyclical movement.[6] In other words, this implies epistemology operating at multiple levels (mesa and meta) and understanding that the production of knowledge already contains a theory of the production of knowledge.[7] This eliminates the question of the anteriority between experience, the process of knowledge production, and self-produced knowledge, but it is understood that all these moments are part of a movement that is in constant transformation. This is perhaps the first research finding that this text examines.

In what follows, the results of the research project on the production of theological knowledge are presented. The research was conducted from 2014 to 2016, in the context of the TSRHR project, funded by the Church of Sweden, and undertaken simultaneously at the Pontificia Universidad Javeriana in Colombia.[8] Methodologically, the research was carried out using the analytical and practical instruments of participatory research; other methods and methodologies were employed as described throughout the text. Here, we describe the experiences throughout the research process, the project development, the two research organizations, and the groups of women with whom the research was carried out. In the end, some final reflections are presented.

About the Processes

The unfolding of a research project over three years comprises a set of processes and contexts that are often not considered or go unnoticed until

6. See Gastellú Camp, *Como espiral de vida.*

7. Gebara, "As epistemologias teológicas e suas consequências," 31–50.

8. The other texts comprising this publication are outputs of the four research projects conducted at the two institutions (Faculdades EST and Pontificia Universidad Javeriana).

the presentation of findings. Considering that the object of the research in focus is knowledge production itself, the epistemology, its processes and contexts, are fundamental for understanding what can be taken as results. This is especially true because such processes and contexts will interfere with research in unpredictable and sometimes imperceptible ways. In the case of the participatory research method and tools for the systematization of experience adopted in this project, these questions are fundamental for understanding the changes and transformations that have occurred.

Still, it is necessary to consider that even when using these methods and research tools, there are subjective and objective elements, conscious and unconscious, which no process of analysis can capture definitively and globally. The marks and ghosts of rationalist positivism haunt us to "let nothing escape," to be able to account for "everything that happened," and everything that was produced on the path traveled. This is the still very-present universalist pretension of capturing "all reality" translated into data and computable results in predefined mental schemes. The very methodological stance assumed, participatory research, laying its roots in popular education and in theories and pedagogies that take daily life and ordinary life as their epistemological venues, requires that we work using perspectives that include instability, ambiguity, combining, provisionality, unpredictability, and the impossibility of cataloging pure and definitive results—just like life itself. Selective narratives are assumed to be a way of producing knowledge that is not an end in itself, but that opens itself up to other processes of learning, theorization, and conceptualization that go beyond it, but are of no less importance. In other words, it is a bet on the possibility of committed research.

In this sense, the research process becomes an experience that acquires significance and will affect the construction of knowledge. In some ways, these are exemplary experiences that motivate reflection and provoke the imagination in relation to what they could be, in relation to real and possible changes and transformations. Without pretending to explain or ascribe a definitive character to a given experience and considering the plurality and diversity of subjects involved in the research process and the way in which each and every one experiences it, the experiences are presented as metaphors that retain their connection with reality. At the same time, they point to other processes and experiences that they can trigger themselves, as they are no longer what they once were and are unrepeatable. In any case, the "experience" category, as already widely discussed and developed in the theoretical fields mentioned, is the fundamental element for understanding the research carried out and the lessons learned. As Oscar Jara states:

> Systematization is that critical interpretation of one or several experiences that, from their ordering and reconstruction, discovers or explains the logic and the meaning of the process experienced in them: the various factors that intervened, how they related to each other, and why they did so. The Systematization of Experiences produces meaningful knowledge and learning that makes it possible to critically appropriate the experiences (their knowledge and feelings), to understand them theoretically and to guide them into the future with a transformative perspective.[9]

In an earlier text, published in the journal "Coisas do Gênero,"[10] a narrative of the initial process of the research was presented. It examined experiences in different contexts and with different subjects. It mentions the Theology and HIV/AIDS project conducted from 2010 to 2012, as a predecessor to the current TSRHR project. It reflects on the construction of the research project itself, as well as the production, relationships, and challenges that emerged from the experience. That text concluded:

> In the epistemological itineraries for research on sexual and reproductive health and rights to be developed within the framework of participatory research, the experiences prior to the research itself become relevant. The research team, the Gender and Religion Program, the Gender Research Group, the Study Group, the funding agency, the partner executing agency, and groups and organizations working on the themes of the research and academic procedures, did not just represent elements of a bureaucratic process. They shaped up as relevant experiences in the elaboration of concepts and methodologies that are already a production of knowledge rooted in each experience, which are connected and deepened with elements of bibliographical research. In this sense, the fundamental element to reflect on the epistemological itineraries resides in the fact that it is a process of a collective and dialogical nature, involving multiple subjects and their own situations.[11]

The text also mentions the first contacts with the two organizations with which the research was conducted during 2015: the Coletivo Feminino Plural and the Fundação Luterana de Diaconia. Contacts with the third

---

9. Jara Holliday, *A sistematização de experiências*, 84.

10. Musskopf et al., "Itinerários epistemológicos."

11. Musskopf et al., "Itinerários epistemológicos," 165.

group, composed of women from the Comunidade Evangélica Floresta Imperial, occurred later, in 2016. Still, in the case of the two organizations and the women's group, it stands out from a methodological viewpoint that "Prior acquaintanceship among the project coordinator and members of the organizations, due to the participation in activities and common circles of relationships, facilitated the first informal surveying contacts, which were important for the construction of the research project"[12] and its unfolding as a whole, particularly in establishing a relationship of mutual trust.

In addition to these actors and contexts, we must also consider that in a research project conducted within the framework of a larger project (TSRHR), a series of other experiences affect and interfere with its trajectory. Over the course of these three years, the primary researcher and the team members have been involved in a set of activities that are described in detail in reports submitted to the Church of Sweden. These activities are not directly linked to the research undertaken, but they constitute experiences that bring important contributions to the research. In summary, the following are mentioned: academic activities (curricular components offered and orientation of academic papers), participation in and organization of academic events (lectures, congresses), participation in various discussion forums on the project themes (local, national, and international), extension activities (workshops, courses), and the preparation of publications. All of these activities involve study and preparation, as well as dialogue with diverse audiences, who enrich and deepen the research itself.

One of the exemplary experiences that had a significant influence on the research process was an extension activity carried out with a group of women in the city of Santo Cristo, in the state of Rio Grande do Sul in Brazil. Women of different ages and backgrounds participated, including women from the local community, civil society groups, and organizations in the region. The proposal was to work on the issue of sexual and reproductive health and rights, including the perspective of religion. After some introductory dynamics of sensitization and discussions on the theme, the suggestion was made to read a biblical text to reflect on the question of religion.

Using the methodology of popular reading of the Bible, the text of the annunciation (Luke 1:26–38) was read to the participants. Their impressions were discussed. In the words of the women, many of whom were greatly disturbed, Mary's submissive posture was affirmed in relation to

---

12. Musskopf et al., "Itinerários epistemológicos," 166.

an Almighty God with patriarchal features. The women were then invited to retell the text freely, focusing on the actions of Mary in the narrative: the angel appears, Mary is frightened; the angel gives a long explanation, and Mary asks questions; the angel gives another long explanation; and Mary responds to the challenge proposed, and the angel disappears. In the process of retelling and identifying Mary's participation in the narrative, several questions arise: just as many women are frightened when they are approached while walking in the street, Mary is frightened too. She asks questions because she wants to understand what is happening and the purpose of this introduction; in the face of Gabriel's lengthy explanation, she does not seem easily convinced—who knows what might have crossed her mind at that moment? Finally, what is the ultimate role of Mary in the narrative? One of the women, who had spoken very little and seemed rather timid, said in an almost inaudible voice, "she decides." The others were astonished, still fixed on the figure of Mary as the submissive woman who represents the submission required of all women in patriarchal theologies and interpretations. Little by little, the women agreed that this reading might destabilize traditionally constructed gender roles within the framework of Christianity. It permits other religious approaches to sexual and reproductive rights from readings of the Bible.[13]

In Latin America, the Bible provides an important space for the discussion of faith and religiosity. The popular reading of the Bible offers important tools for a theological production that builds on lived realities, including in the field of sexual and reproductive rights. For that reason, the exercise was repeated with the team from the Fundação Luterana de Diaconia and with the women's group of the Comunidade Floresta Imperial; the results were similar.

The experience at Santo Cristo demonstrates another element to be considered in the epistemological itineraries of the research, like those mentioned in relation to the process of elaborating the research project. So many other unforeseen or unimagined experiences are happening in various places and spaces. The richness of the process of systematizing experiences perceives movements like these, which are ancillary to the research undertaken, and projects results beyond the original research scope.

---

13. The Bible reading exercise was inspired by a Catholic campaign on the right to decide, which said, "Even Mary was consulted to be the mother of God—For the legalization and decriminalization of abortion in Latin America and the Caribbean."

About Organizations and Groups

As mentioned above, the research was conducted with three organizations/ groups with distinct characteristics, which will be described next. Follow-up and dialogue with these groups took place within the framework of the project's general objective:

> To analyze ways of producing knowledge about health and rights in the field of sexuality and human reproduction in religious groups and social organizations, based on the instruments developed by liberation theologies, through popular education and participatory research in Latin America, this study articulated contributions from feminist theology and gender studies, with the aim of theological reflection on these themes and the formation of pastoral, social, and political agents capable of implementing forms of liberation in their contexts.[14]

During 2015, after the dialogue and the signing of the Partnership Agreement in 2014,[15] the Coletivo Feminino Plural and the Fundação Luterana de Diaconia came onboard.

The Coletivo Feminino Plural, identified as "a social group/organization with political work in sexual and reproductive health and rights issues,"[16] works for female empowerment, participation in spaces of power and decision, and control over social activities. It participates in reporting and monitoring, provides advice on public policies, teaches courses, and provides training. It is a feminist non-governmental organization, founded in 1996 by a group of women who identified with the struggle for human rights and citizenship of women and girls.[17] That is:

> It acts in the women's movement, by means of local, regional, national, and international networking, joining networks and campaigns, advocating for public policies, compliance with national and international instruments of women's human rights, and the

---

14. This is according to the research project.

15. Musskopf et al., "Itinerários epistemológicos," 165–68.

16. This is according to the research project.

17. This information was from the website, http://femininoplural.org.br/site/quem-somos. At least two other research studies were carried out on the Coletivo Feminino Plural (information received from the members of the Collective). Silva, "Análise das relações entre quadros interpretativos e repertórios de ação em duas organizações feministas"; Silva, "Mulheres em movimento (s)."

end of all forms of violence and discrimination against women and girls.[18]

The Coletivo Feminino Plural has conducted numerous activities, projects, and campaigns grounded in their fundamental principles. Among the projects monitored during the research were Projeto Conexões—Ações Integradas contra HIV/AIDS e Violência de Gênero (Project Connections–Integrated Actions against HIV/AIDS and Gender Violence) [19]; Projeto Girassóis—Gênero e Saúde Mental (Sunflowers Project–Gender and Mental Health) [20]; Centro de Referência para Mulheres Vítimas de Violências Patrícia Esber (Patrícia Esber Reference Center for Women Victims of Violence)[21]; Ponto de Cultura Feminista—Corpo, arte, expressão (Feminist Culture Point—Body, Art, Expression)[22]; and Grupo Inclusivass (Female Inclusive Group).[23] These initiatives reveal the diversity of the topics the organization is involved in, as well as the depth with which they work, responding to contemporary issues and challenges. This work is based on a solid trajectory that simultaneously demonstrates the capacity to identify and incorporate new perspectives that emerge from the reality

18. Available at http://femininoplural.org.br/site/quem-somos (last accessed May 12, 2020)

19. The members of the research team participated in the evaluation of the project, mainly in its closing phase. The information on the project is available at http://conexoescfp.blogspot.com.br/p/quem-somos.html (last accessed March 18, 2020)

20. The team members participated in a seminar on the project theme and in team meetings. Information about the project is available at http://girassoisgenero.blogspot.com.br/ (last accessed March 18, 2020) See also material produced by the project, *O que há de errado com ela?*, a film by Mirela Kruel; Negrão, Rodrigues, & Vargas, 2015; and the workbook, *Precisamos estar sempre bem?*

21. The members of the team visited the center and participated in activities, highlighting action with women from the project *Mulheres Mil* on basic health. Information about the center is available at http://femininoplural.org.br/site/projetos/centro-de-referencia-para-mulheres-vitimas-de-violencia-patricia-esber-canoasrs .

22. The team members participated in the decentralized project activities. The research coordinator lectured at the panel *Corpo, autonomia e expressão numa perspectiva feminista* on June 10, on the agenda of Feminarium *"Por uma cultura feminista: transformar o mundo transformando a si mesmos."* Information is available at http://femininoplural.org.br/site/projetos/ponto-de-cultura-feminista-corpo-arte-e-expressao and https://pontodeculturafeminista.wordpress.com/(last accessed March 18, 2020).

23. The team members followed the actions of the group, spoke with the coordinator, and participated in the development of the materials (film and booklet). Information on the group is available at http://inclusivass.blogspot.com.br/ (last accessed March 18, 2020). The questions regarding the *Inclusivass* Group will be explored below.

in which the organization is involved, and to deal with the challenges of being a non-governmental organization, particularly from the viewpoint of sustainability.

The Fundação Luterana de Diaconia (FLD), identified as a "group/organization linked to religious issues with discussion in the area of gender and sexuality,"[24] is linked to the Evangelical Church of Lutheran Confession in Brazil (IECLB). The organization was founded in 2010, and the Council is made up of representatives of the Synods of the Church.[25] Its mission is:

> To support and monitor programs and projects of organized civil
> society groups that strengthen the protagonism of people and their
> communities, promoting quality of life, citizenship, and social
> justice [and as vision] to be a reference between national and in-
> ternational partners in the area of project methodology and social
> management, supporting people in the defense of their rights and
> in building inclusive and sustainable communities, where they can
> meet their basic needs, while respecting the environment.[26]

The FLD has as its thematic areas Diaconia, Human Rights, Socio-Environmental Justice, Economic Justice, and Humanitarian Aid; and, as crosscutting themes, gender justice, protagonism, and overcoming violence and prejudices.

In addition to supporting projects, the organization also conducts projects and activities,[27] including *Rede de Comércio Justo e Solidário*,[28] *Catadoras e Catadores em Rede—Fortalecendo a Reciclagem Popular*,[29]

24. This is according to the research project.

25. The "Synods" are part of the organizational structure of the IECLB, and the Constitution of the IECLB states: "Art. 15–The Synod, as a religious organization, is made up of the whole set of communities and parishes of a specific geographical area. It has the task of planning and energizing the ecclesiastical work in its area, deciding on the way the Church manifests itself in the concretization of its purposes and executing the directives and goals established in the council, in compliance with the provisions of Art. 7°." Available athttp://www.luteranos.com.br/conteudo_organizacao/governanca-suporte-normativo/constituicao-da-ieclb-1 (last accessed March 18, 2020)

26. The information is available at http://fld.com.br/page/missao-e-visao/ (last accessed March 18, 2020)

27. The team members participated in several meetings of the organization's team, where the activities of the various projects were presented.

28. The members of the team participated in the training activities and network assembly. The latter also participated in the IV Latin American Congress of Gender and Religion. More information on the project is available at http://comerciojustofld.com.br/.

29. The team members participated in activities with representatives of the groups.

Mulher Catadora é Mulher que Luta,[30] *Nem Tão Doce Lar,*[31] and *Rede de Diaconia.*[32] The projects carried out by FLD also cover diverse areas and themes. This diversity is even more evident in the projects supported by the organization, especially through the Small Projects Program.[33] What is not always evident, and is a subject of discussion in the organization itself and of this research, is the "religious" bond or even the theological perspective implied in the actions performed.

The third group, identified as "a grassroots group linked to a religious institution for which [it was proposed] the discussion on sexual and reproductive health and rights connected to religious and theological issues,"[34] was monitored during 2016. It is a discussion group formed with the specific purpose of participating in the research.

The Comunidade Floresta Imperial is a community within the IECLB, which has recently completed 50 years of existence in the city of Novo Hamburgo in the Brazilian state of Rio Grande do Sul. The Comunidade Floresta Imperial is constituted mainly of industrial workers who migrated to the city, and today it has more than 2,000 members. Being in an urban space, it is involved with the problems of its context, and is recognized for its actions in the field of education and social assistance, through the AssociaçãoBeneficenteEvangélica da Floresta Imperial, responsible for the ColégioSinodal da Paz, Escola Infantil da Paz, Lar Padilha, and Ação Encontro.[35] However, it also preserves specific characteristics of more rural communities, as many of the people who frequent it maintain ties with the countryside.

More information about the project is available at http://fld.com.br/catadores/catadores/index.html.

30. The team members followed the development of the project and conducted initial training with the team on sexual rights and reproductive rights. More information about the project is available at http://fld.com.br/mulhercatadora/.

31. The members of the team participated in training events and facilities at the exhibition, which was also set up at the IV Latin American Congress on Gender and Religion. More information about the project is available at http://fld.com.br/page/nem-tao-doce-lar/.

32. The members of the team participated in regional and national meetings of the network, workshops, and courses with institutions connected to the network. More information about the project is available at http://rededeiaconia.com.br/.

33. More information is available at http://fld.com.br/page/programa-de-pequenos-projetos/.

34. This is according to the research project.

35. "Comunidade Floresta Imperial."

The groups that participated in the research have quite different characteristics; and the experiences with each had their own particularities. Although the monitoring of activities was based on the agenda and on the interests of each organization and group, the question that led this research was: how is knowledge production developed and experienced in each space? Experiences included those of members of the organizations and their groups' daily routines, as well as the issues raised by the presence of members of the research team.

With the first two organizations, the goal was to understand their processes of knowledge production in their field of action, as well as to unleash processes of knowledge production based on how they dealt with the themes proposed by the project. In the third group, the central objective was to initiate processes of production of theological knowledge on health and sexual rights and reproductive rights. In the background was the fact that it is a group of active people/women in a religious community that carries out activities in the presence of a pastor; we paid attention to their processes of knowledge production and the knowledge produced during the research.

The experiences were diverse and surprising enough that the transformation processes unleashed in the research team, as well as in the organizations and groups, did not end immediately. Things continued to unfold after the formal finalization of the research. Nevertheless, the systematization of the experiences accomplished allows us to perceive significant elements that were not conclusive, but which can be used to further thinking about producing theological knowledge on sexual and reproductive health and rights, and their impact on people's lives, communities, and society as a whole.

Activities Developed with the Organizations and Groups

The research process presented here occurred in four different periods. The first focused on deepening the bibliographical survey. At the same time, the first contacts were made with the organizations and groups. The second period was characterized by the monitoring of two organizations. This monitoring process involved participation in activities carried out by the organizations, but also in training activities with the organizations, groups, and projects they developed. The third period focused on the work developed with the Grupo da Comunidade Floresta Imperial, with a formative character, but against the background of the construction of knowledge by the women using popular education and popular reading of the Bible. In the fourth period, the data collected were systematized from the perspective of the systematization of the experiences.[36]

The data and materials collected during the activities were used during the systematization. In order to record the activities and reflections initiated at the moment of participation or in the conversations of team members (on the way to and from the activities), a field diary was used. In addition, the materials available at and produced by the organizations and groups were collected. The activities were recorded in photographic images, which constitute another source of research data.[37] The information recorded in the field journal was later systematized in a registration table constructed according to Oscar Jara's book.[38] With all of this material gathered, the team held meetings to analyze these materials, recounting each one of the activities, reviewing the materials and photographs, and identifying the elements pertinent to the research objectives.[39] In this pro-

36. Throughout the TSRHR project, different moments of team training occurred. On November 4 and 5, 2014, the "Brazil-Colombia Interchange Seminar on Theology and Sexuality, Reproductive Health and Rights" took place with the participation of Professor Dr. Edla Eggert, who discussed methodology, dynamics, and evaluation with the teams during the participatory research process with the groups involved. On March 19 and 20, 2015, the "II Seminar on Theology and Gender" took place at the Pontificia Universidad Javeriana in Bogotá, where methodological issues in PAR (Participatory Action Research) were also discussed. In the same year, on April 6 and 10, 2015, in São Leopoldo, the extension course "Popular Education, Participatory Research, and Systematization of Experiences" took place. The educator and sociologist Dr. Oscar Jara, facilitated this with the goal of qualifying and building the capacity of professors and students for the training of researchers from the perspective of PAR, based on historical questions, concepts, and characteristics of popular education. On October 4 and 11, 2016, the training seminar, "Systematizations and Analyses: A methodological construction in process," was held with the assistance of Prof. Dr. Edla Eggert.

37. Although the collected materials and photographic records were from the process of systematizing experiences and used as complementary data for rerecording the experiences, they were not analyzed separately or in-depth. Instead, they were formatted as a source that can be used in future studies, and a first exercise was performed by Rebeca Lahass, using the concept of "Photoethnography" (Achutti, *Fotoetnografia*).

38. Jara, *A sistematização de experiências*, 77–78, 108–10.

39. In the first half of 2016, the research carried out with the Coletivo Feminino Plural (CFP) began with a survey of the activities monitored, including the preparation of the texts and an analysis of materials, as well as a survey of the activities by the Fundação Luterana de Diaconia (FLD). Four team meetings took place during the first half of 2016 to systematize the experiences of the Coletivo Feminino Plural (January 11, March 4, March 16, and May 3). In the second semester, three team meetings took place to systematize the experiences of the follow-up activities of the Fundação Luterana de

cess, the activities experienced with the organizations and groups, besides the lived experiences, have become "formative experiences"[40] in the sense that the team itself underwent a formation process grounded in the experiences lived with these organizations and groups.

Coletivo Feminino Plural

The members of the team participated in 34 activities with the Coletivo Feminino Plural. These activities included visits, conversations, and participation in meetings with members of the organization's and project's team. There were also public activities in which the organization was involved or promoted, and activities developed within the scope of the projects executed by the organization. In addition, in at least four activities, the research team developed and participated in training activities with the Coletivo. Throughout this process, the underlying epistemological elements were identified in the organization's work on health and sexual and reproductive rights. References to theology and religious articulations were also presented.

In epistemological terms, it is possible to affirm that the Coletivo Feminino Plural understands itself as a producer of knowledge. It is identified with and substantiated in diverse feminist theories and studies. In addition to the trajectory and individual training of its members (as well as volunteers and the project team), it also promotes the creation of spaces for study, formation, training, and research, both with the Coletivo and through its projects and activities that tend to include this educative aspect in their proposals. This is evidenced, for example, in the wide production of materials ranging from campaign and educational materials (such as booklets, folders, and leaflets) to audiovisual materials (films and videos) and bibliographic production (texts, articles, and books).

Diaconia (June 24, September 2, and October 3). In January 2017, two meetings took place to systematize the experiences of working with the women's group of Novo Hamburgo (January 6 and 24). In the meetings of the team, DataShow was used to project the tables with the notes about the activities, which were reread and retold, and photographs were taken during each activity and materials collected. In this way, it was possible to "relive" those experiences and highlight the learning of each of them individually and as a whole. After this exercise, the team members were challenged to write about the dynamics of the systematization meetings, learn from the organizations, and share their impressions from the photographs and materials. This was all considered in the preparation of this text.

40. Josso, *Experiências de vida e formação.*

In its epistemological assumptions, the importance of women's experiences was identified from the outset. Women are the public that makes up the organization and with which the organization works. In this respect, the diversity of experiences and women with whom the Coletivo works is highlighted, reflecting the political and theoretical perspectives of contemporary feminism. It is from the experiences of the women who work in the Coletivo, and from the diverse women with whom the Coletivo operates that knowledge is produced about this reality and with the objective of transforming its violent, oppressive, and exclusionary aspects. For this same reason, another fundamental aspect in the production of knowledge engendered by the Coletivo is the dialogic and participatory perspective that is evident in its practice. This is expressed through the sharing of decisions about the actions, activities, and materials produced in team meetings, assemblies, and gatherings in various modalities.

One thing that drew attention to the actions developed by and with the Coletivo Feminino Plural during 2015 was their use of different languages in the processes of knowledge production triggered by their activities and forms of diffusion. There is a strong presence of art and culture, both in the creation of the visual identity of the organization and its materials, in the activities developed, and in the way the Coletivo presents itself in public spaces. Although this approach has been emphasized by the realization of the Project Ponto de Cultura Feminista and the various activities it developed, the artisanal and artistic production (including the official banner of the organization) is generally noticeable and carries a deeply embodied and performative component, which is historically rooted in the organization and its political and pedagogical activities.

Two interrelated issues, however, should be highlighted in the observation of the epistemological elements generatedby the organization. Among them is the fact that, even though there is a well-defined plan, agenda, and purpose, the organization lives under the contingency of access to financial resources for its actions (experienced by all non-governmental organizations). This often means aligning work proposals to calls for proposals from governmental and non-governmental funding agencies. This issue relates to the strong public presence of the Coletivo (in networks, forums, commissions, and political actions) to the extent that the Coletivo itself participates in the process of setting specific agendas and themes that are important to the lives of women, but they also seek to respond to demands that arise from this same presence in public spaces. Thus, while these elements can be seen as conditioning the organization's actions, the way it deals with them also reveals a high capacity to handle urgencies and emergencies, in terms of organizational flexibility, mobilizing networks, and producing relevant content. In epistemological terms, issues such as improvisation and adaptability in the face of diverse situations proved to be important in the processes of knowledge production unleashed by the organization. Such processes were the result of the dynamic and diverse agendas that mark daily life.

Finally, this public presence also guarantees and promotes another element considered fundamental in the production of knowledge: networking between the experiences lived in the grassroots work, the political action, and the dialogue with public agents in the area of public policies and the academic discussion with universities and research groups. It is in this "mandala"[41] of relationships, and the experiences lived in it that knowledge is being produced in the context of the Coletivo Feminino Plural.

Regarding the production of theological knowledge or the incorporation of theological or religious questions in the work developed by the Coletivo Feminino Plural, it was noticed that the research project and the presence of the research team promoted fruitful dialogue. The Feminário[42] promoted by the project Ponto de Cultura Feminista, for example, provided an opportunity to present the contributions of feminist theology to this debate.[43] At the launch of the Coletivo Feminino Plural's Study Group, it

41. The mandala figure has been evoked by the Gender and Religion Program of Faculdades EST since its restructuring (from 2013), in its understanding of the process of producing academic knowledge. In the project developed by Musskopf and Blasi, 2017, they argued: "By definition, the Gender and Religion Program is a space for networking. In general, it networks with civil society and social movements, with governments and bodies responsible for public administration and religious institutions, for the implementation of its initiatives. As part of an Institution of Higher Education, it carries out its activities in the various areas of Theology (Biblical, Practical, Historical-Systematic, Education and Religion), and in the various courses and programs of the institution through Extension, Teaching, and Research. It is understood that these three dimensions must be deeply interconnected, in order to fulfill the objectives and goals, following Oscar Jara's suggestion: 'instead of thinking about this relationship as linear and hierarchical, it is necessary to see it from the perspective of three interdependent and equally important axes, as a 'mandala'." See: "Oscar Jara e as fronteiras da extensão" http://www.ufrgs.br/prorext-siteantigo/news/oscar-jara-e-as-fronteiras-da-extensao.

42. "Feminário" is a word coined by the group as a version of "Seminário" (Seminar) in its feminine form.

43. On June 10, 2015, in the context of the "Feminário for a Feminist Culture," promoted by Ponto de Cultura, André S. Musskopf spoke on the theme "Body, autonomy,

called attention to the fact that in an opening performance that highlighted women who had contributed to the field of feminism, one of the personalities mentioned was Ivone Gebara, a Brazilian feminist theologian.[44] At a panel discussion during the Seminar on Transformational Diakonia, organized by the Fundação Luterana de Diaconia, the coordinator of the Coletivo Feminino Plural spoke of feminist movements and, in her speech, mentioned the importance of re-reading religion and theology, more specifically the biblical texts, to destabilize fundamentalist religious discourse. She highlighted the positive role that theology and religion can play as allies with social movements.[45] These are some examples of how elements of theology and religion were included in the organization's discussions and concerns. The continuation of partnership and collaboration will surely deepen these constructions.

The more concrete results from the point of view of knowledge production through participatory research may have occurred in the dialogue with the Grupo Inclusivass for women with disabilities, linked to the Coletivo Feminino Plural. Also noteworthy is the work of the Research Assistant Luciana Steffen, whose doctoral research topic relates theology, gender, feminism, and disability. Her thesis project was also profoundly influenced by this contact and joint work.[46] The subtitling (in Spanish and English) and the audio description (in Portuguese) of the short film "Carol,"[47] was

and expression in the perspective of Feminist Theology." The activity took place at the Mário Quintana House of Culture (Porto Alegre, RS), and the presentation presented the theoretical and methodological proposals of feminist theology in its various forms, demonstrating the progress in this area, and highlighting the question of the "body" and "embodiment" for feminist theological reflection. For many participants, hearing about feminist theology was a novelty.

44. The launch of the Study Group took place on September 30 at the Porto Alegre Culture Club. Luisa Gabriela and Carolina Pommer (coordinator and member, respectively) of the administrative committee of the Ponto de Cultura Feminista: Corpo, Arte e Expressão presented the performance mentioned above.

45. The Seminar "Transforming Diaconia and Human Rights" took place on October 1 at the Salesian House in Porto Alegre. Representatives of Haitian immigrants, the National Movement of Collectors of Recyclable Materials, the Landless Movement, the Movement of Dam-Affected People, and the Movement of Unemployed Workers also participated in the Social Movements Table.

46. The following texts were produced by the doctoral candidate during the research period: Steffen and Musskopf, "Direitos sexuais e direitos reprodutivos das pessoas com deficiências"; Steffen and Santos, "As Inclusivass"; Steffen, "Refletindo sobre Gênero."

47. The film was produced by Mirela Kruel. It tells the life story of Elisandra Carolina dos Santos, a coordinator of the Inclusivass Group, and was nominated for and won

supported by the TSSRD Project and the research team participated in the production of the booklet "Women with Disabilities: Sexual and Reproductive Rights," including a section on "Disability, Feminism, and Religion."[48] The Inclusivass Group, the Coletivo Feminino Plural, and the research team were involved in several activities related to both the film and booklet.

Although the film does not explicitly address the theme of religion, the involvement in the subtitling/audio description process and subsequently in activities to promote and distribute the film allowed a closer relationship with the Inclusivass Group and its coordinator (Elisandra Carolina dos Santos), as well as the inclusion of religious and theological issues in dialogue and activities. The result of this was also the inclusion of these discussions in the booklet. In discussion with the team responsible for developing the material, the possibility of including theological and religious discourse on the various topics was raised. The inclusion of an Inclusivass-led Bible study that dealt with these issues was also considered. However, when presenting the material to the group, several questions were raised about the presence of themes and reflections on religion in the material. It was decided to include a session that dealt exclusively with this theme. In this sense, we attempted to present the theme in a broad and open manner, offering information that might challenge people to think about these themes, as follows:

> Religions are constituted through traditions, sacred texts, myths, rites, and symbols that refer to the experience of people with dimensions of the sacred, transcendence, and deities. These materialize in discourses and practices that can take the form of dogmas, doctrines, and regulations/rules. Reflections on gender, sexual rights, and reproductive rights pose important challenges for religions and their theological constructions.[49]

Although there was interest and curiosity on the part of the Coletivo Feminino Plural in relation to feminist approaches to religion and theology, there was some resistance to inserting this subject into the daily life of the organization. On the one hand, it has always been clear that resistance was the result of previous negative experiences, especially as religious discourses and practices have historically been against women's rights in general, and sexual and reproductive rights, specifically. This continues to

awards at several film festivals (*Carol*, 2016).

48. Grupo Inclusivass, *Mulheres com deficiência*.

49. Grupo Inclusivass, *Mulheres com deficiência*, 21.

be a commonly held perception, not only in the Coletivo but also in feminist movements in general. Such a perception is undoubtedly part of the damage caused by sexist and patriarchal religious discourses that have prevented approximation with theology and religious experiences that depart from presuppositions and that promote alternative frameworks.

In a certain sense, this reveals that these productions and practices in the field of theology and religion have not reached these spaces. There are several reasons for this (including conservative institutions and ideals making them invisible). In any case, the organization's difficulty and resistance to these issues are also due to a lack of knowledge about feminist production in this area; this is reflected in prudence and (possibly exaggerated) fear around putting these issues on the agenda. Nonetheless, the bonds of affection and trust created throughout the research will be crucial for other approaches and dialogue to take place, so that these themes can be worked out in more depth later. There is no doubt, however, that collaboration in the development of this project has impacted and transformed both the organization and the research team. Their forms of knowledge production contribute to new theological knowledge in the field of health and sexual and reproductive rights.

Fundação Luterana de Diaconia

While developing the research with the Fundação Luterana de Diaconia, the team members participated in 28 activities, visits, and meetings with leaders of the organization. In addition to team-based activities developed within the scope of the organization's projects and activities, the focus of the research with this group was to perceive and elaborate on the organization's epistemological elements for the production of knowledge about health and sexual and reproductive rights. In this case, we considered that this is an organization with religious connections. Thus, the focus was more on perceiving how these themes (sexual and reproductive health and rights) are treated, based on the theology and religion in the actions developed and supported by the organization.

At the beginning of the research process, the institution already had a history of discussing gender issues, especially in the framework of the construction and approval of an Institutional Gender Justice Policy.[50] Accompanied by the Code of Conduct,[51] this document, and the process that

50. Fundação Luterana de Diaconia, *Política de Justiça de Gênero*.

51. The Code of Conduct makes direct reference to the Gender Justice Policy and

led to its adoption seems to have represented a significant milestone in the organization's trajectory in these themes.Gender justice also includes issues of sexual and reproductive health and rights, and was incorporated into all of the activities developed by the organization.[52] Other activities and projects, such as the traveling exhibition "*Nem Tão Doce Lar*"(Not so sweet home), prominently included the gender issue. Since the first contact with the organization, however, the emphasis has been on the desire to more consistently deepen and broaden the discussion of sexual and reproductive health and rights.

Both the institutional documents (Gender Justice Policy and Code of Conduct) and the project *Nem Tão Doce Lar* reveal important epistemological issues in the theological knowledge produced by the organization in the area of sexual and reproductive health and rights. In the case of both documents, the collective and participatory drafting up until their approval by the Assembly, the intentionality that underlies them, and the theological reflections they contain were highlighted. As documents—which reflect institutional policies—their application in the various spheres to which they are attached, places the related themes on the organization's agenda, both in its management and in the actions, it develops and supports, in a transversal way.

In terms of theological reflection, the Gender Justice Policy, for example, generates biblical and denominational issues articulated with the concept of "Diakonia":

> Biblical understanding of the creation of the human being indicates an equal empowerment for women and men. Prophetic, political, and transformative Diakonia must denounce any imbalance of power that causes inequalities and exclusions, motivated by the androcentric values of patriarchy. Diakonia is liberating, transforming action; it is an action of impact on the realities and groups that live economic, cultural, sexist, racist, homophobic, and environmental oppressions.[53]

seeks to curb "sexual abuse and exploitation of children and adolescents, sexual harassment, bullying, racism and homophobia" as violations of "rights based on gender, religion, class, generation, sexual orientation, and environmental realities" (Fundação Luterana de Diaconia, Code of Conduct).

52. At all the events and activities organized and promoted by FLD, the participants have access to the Gender Justice Policy and Code of Conduct and sign a commitment to comply with them. In addition, a provision is made for channels for reporting and monitoring in the event of a breach of the principles set out therein.

53. Fundação Luterana de Diaconia, *Política de Justiça de Gênero*, 15.

48

In the project, *Nem Tão Doce Lar*, the production of knowledge about domestic violence and related issues present different dimensions. The setting up of the exhibition, for example, depends on the articulation of local networks (preferably including churches and religious groups) and the provision of training for volunteer greeters.[54] According to the description of the project:

> *Nem Tão Doce Lar* involves a methodology of collective intervention to overcome family violence. An itinerant exhibition makes it possible to popularize the discussion and the confrontation of violence by bringing into the public space a typical family home, with information and images that denounce the violence suffered by women, children, and young people.[55]

The training offered to greeters is in the form of dialog workshops on topics such as the concept and types of violence (religious violence), definition of and information about gender inequality, cycles of violence, legislation, care for victims, children and adolescents, homosexuality and sexual diversity, and information on the exhibition, and the role of a greeter.[56] In training, religion and theology appear in the discussion on religious violence[57] and in reference to feminist theology, which promotes gender equity and justice, and identifies violence with sin.

Regarding the assembly of the exhibition, the manual provided by the organization states that:

> The exhibition consists of assembling the replica of a house, with furniture, household utensils, and objects that refer to the issue

54. According to the materials made available by the Coordinator of the Project Rogério Aguiar, it is the responsibility of the greeters to "orient the visit, stay alert, make yourself available for dialog, and say where to seek assistance, and record impressions and reflections."—"Thus, workshops for the greeters were introduced, significantly increasing the number of people trained both to organize the exhibition and to welcome and to converse with the visitors." Menezes, "Nem Tão Doce Lar," 193.

55. Nem Tão Doce Lar. http://fld.com.br/page/nem-tao-doce-lar/.

56. The information was taken from materials provided by the Project Coordinator, Rogério Aguiar. See also, Menezes, *Nem tão doce lar*, the bibliographic material produced by FLD and used in the training.

57. According to material used in the training, "Religious violence: occurs when biblical/theological aspects are used to justify violent actions in the domestic sphere. Often the Bible is used to blame women for the evils of the world and to make them invisible, making it difficult for them to leave violent relationships and legitimize their oppression." This definition is contrasted with the biblical passage, "For freedom Christ has set us free. Stand firm and do not submit again to the yoke of bondage" (Gal 6:11).

of violence. Inside the house are used posters with pictures and data on violence . . . as a form of denunciation, it is important to put objects in the house that are commonly used by attackers. . . . What other "clues" could represent violence in the exhibition? The littered bed, objects lying on the floor, broken toys, dolls without heads . . . Next to the objects should be placed the posters with information about the violence.[58]

The Assembly Manual makes no specific reference to theology or religion. In some arrangements, however, one can see religious elements, such as the inclusion of Bibles or other materials related to churches. Its assembly in religious communities and the participation of religious leaders in the process of assembling the exhibition, however, has the potential to produce theological reflections and religious practices that re-signify the issues raised by the exhibition.

It is also important to mention that the emergence of the exhibition and its development in the Brazilian context are closely related to discussion of the exhibition themes in the religious context. According to Marilu Nörnberg Menezes:

Nem Tão Doce Lar was born from an international exhibition called Rua das Rosas, created by the German anthropologist Una Hombrecher, with the support of the agency Bread for the World (BFW). The initial proposal, still in a European language, was presented in Porto Alegre, Rio Grande do Sul, Brazil, from February 14 to 23, 2016, during the 9th Assembly of the World Council of Churches (WCC). It consisted of a replica of a house in which furniture, household goods, images, and data pointed to the context of domestic violence. At that time, it was part of the effort of the WCC itself and member churches within the framework of the [UNESCO] Decade of Overcoming Violence.[59]

In this passage, one notices the search for the contextualization of the proposal, which continues to happen each time it is assembled, acquiring specific features and elements according to the local reality. In theological terms, even if this is not always explicit in the exposition itself, the proposal is based on the concept of "Diakonia" adopted by the organization. In this regard:

58. This was taken from materials provided by the Project Coordinator, Rogério Aguiar.

59. Menezes, "Nem Tão Doce Lar," 190–91.

Diakonia is a word derived from the Greek used in the Bible, in the New Testament, with different meanings. Sometimes it refers to material help specific to people in need. At other times, it means serving the tables and, at others, it refers to the distribution of financial resources. Also, in contemporary theology, the word Diakonia has a diversity of connotations and representations. For the FLD, Diakonia means serving to change people's lives, in order to contribute to the construction of citizenship for the less favored.[60]

That is, in terms of theological epistemology, the *Nem Tão Doce Lar* project rests on what is called "diaconal methodology: focused on transformative action."[61] Rooted in the biblical concept of "Diakonia," the project produces knowledge from the experience of the people involved, in a collective, participatory, and contextualized way. It brings together several actors and uses information produced in the context of feminism, gender studies, and theology.

During the research process, and possibly also motivated by it, themes related to sexual and reproductive health and rights were approached in several of the organization's venues. Projects supported by the organization became important spaces to explore research themes. In 2015, for the Call for Small Projects on human rights, the issue of sexual and reproductive rights was explicitly included.[62] In this sense, support for projects in this area, and the relationships established with the partners, are another factor that has influenced the organization's production of knowledge on the themes. They foreground these themes and receive input from the projects that address them. In addition, within the scope of theological reflection, it is possible to assume that the relationship established through project support represents an important element, be it in the case of projects developed by groups with religious ties, or by the "religious" character of the supporting organization, from the elaboration around the concept of "Diakonia."

Another project in which the research team was involved was the Diakonia Network.[63] Team members were invited to present the research

60. Fundação Luterana de Diaconia, *Código de conduta*; Menezes, "Nem Tão Doce Lar," 187.

61. This is according to materials provided by the Project Coordinator, Rogério Aguiar.

62. Fundação Luterana de Diaconia, *Balanço Celebrativo FLD*.

63. The Diakonia Network is formed of diaconate institutions linked to the Evangelical Lutheran Confession Church in Brazil (IECLB).

project in the Network meetings.[64] The presentation of the research project, in general, and in the meetings, provoked interest among the participants, who stated that these are important topics for discussion in their institutions. As a result, a course on Gender and Aging[65] was held with one of the institutions, as well as a workshop at the regional meeting of the Network.[66] At the beginning of the research, the project was also presented at the organization's General Assembly and it was well received.[67]

Even though in those spaces the research project was presented fundamentally, i.e. with no specific action or discussion of the themes, they were understood as spaces of formation, where participants were awakened to these themes in an institutional context. Likewise, it was formative to have research team members participate in meetings with the organization's team (including those working on various projects). This was the case in the team meeting held in 2014,[68] prior to the signing of the Term of Commitment, and especially at the meeting held on June 25, 2015. At the 2015 meeting, in addition to presenting historical and conceptual issues related to sexual and reproductive health and rights, a dynamic was developed with a biblical text from Luke 1:26–38 (Annunciation), following the methodology adopted by the group in Santo Cristo. Here again, the process of re/reading the text provoked oddity and surprise among

64. The meetings took place on April 16, 2015, in Florianópolis, with institutions in Santa Catarina and Paraná; on April 24, 2015 in Novo Hamburgo, with institutions of Rio Grande do Sul; and on June 17–18, 2015, in Florianópolis, with institutions from Rio Grande do Sul, Santa Catarina, and Paraná.

65. The course "Gender and Aging" was part of a project carried out by *Lar Recanto do Sossego* with the support of the Fundação Luterana de Diaconia. Through this project, the workers of the government of Trombudo Central and neighboring municipalities were given training on the concepts of gender, sex, and sexuality, and on the sociocultural impact of affirming the dignity of each resident who is cared for in the social welfare referral centers. The course, coordinated by Marcia Blasi, was developed with advice from Luciana Steffen, Elisa Schroder, Ilze Zirbel, and Marli Brun.

66. At the meeting held on June 17–18, 2015, the Project Research Assistant, Luciana Steffen, and the Research Assistant of the Gender and Religion Program, DaniéliBusanelloKrob, delivered the workshop "Gender Justice: Gender and Music."

67. The assembly took place on March 23, 2015 in São Leopoldo.

68. At the meeting, held on January 12, 2014, the participants were presented with four words on paper cards: health, rights, sexuality, and reproduction. The participants were invited to choose two of the four words and form groups from the choices to talk about the relationship between them and the motivation for choosing them. Through the discussion raised by this exercise, which deepened the themes and concepts, the research project was presented.

many participants. The process proposed ways of dealing with the research themes from a theological/religious perspective. The question remained how to incorporate these issues into the activities carried out in the daily life of the organization.[69]

What has drawn attention since the beginning of the research with this organization is that the relationship of these themes from the perspective of religion or theology is not always evident. In the very first meeting, when the research proposal was presented to the team, some members were surprised that the Fundação Luterana de Diaconia was identified as an organization "with religious ties." As it is involved and conducts projects in various social spaces and themes, and not all members of the team have an educational background in this area, the theme of religion and the discussion of a theological perspective is not always present for those who work in the institution. It is suspected that this question, raised a few times by the research team, has been deepened throughout the research process, particularly through the concept of "transformative Diakonia." Although this concept was already being employed, it gained strength during the period in which the organization was accompanied by the researchers. The concept was more explicitly in the activities and materials produced during the celebration of its fifteenth anniversary. According to one of these materials:

> Transformative Diakonia is a concept that mobilizes the reflection and action of the Fundação Luterana de Diaconia (FLD), which aims to generate a circularity of liberation, transformation, and incidence. We confess and believe in a Diakonia that promotes collective actions in realities and groups that experience economic, social, political, cultural, sexist, racist, xenophobic, homo-lesbo-transphobic, and environmental oppression. In the text of Mark 12:30, Jesus points out that love is the heart of Diakonia, in establishing the first commandment of love.[70]

The very name of the seminar held on the celebration of the organization's fifteenth anniversary made the emphasis on this concept explicit.[71]

69. At another time in the training, with the team that conducted the project *Mulher Catadora é Mulher que Luta* held on May 5, 2015, the debate also centered on a discussion of the history and concepts related to health and sexual and reproductive rights, leaving the question about a theological/religious approach to this question open, even though their team was very interested in discussing this further.

70. Fundação Luterana de Diaconia, *Balanço Celebrativo FLD*, 7.

71. As mentioned above, the seminar, Transformative Diakonia and Human Rights, occurred on October 1, at the Salesianas House in Porto Alegre.

In its programming, it is noteworthy that two female theologians participated in the initial Roundtable "Diakonia transformational dialogue."[72] The panelists presented historical and conceptual discussions in the field of theology and religion to an audience formed by the FLD team, members of projects supported by the organization, partners of other organizations, and other guests. Perhaps it was here, more clearly and concretely, that the "religious tie" and the production of knowledge in the theological field appeared, even in the relationship with sexual and reproductive health and rights.

Another element that appeared in the celebration of the 15th anniversary of the organization and which is present at various moments in the activities that followed is the celebratory and meditative elements of the organization's work. In the context of the commemoration of the 15th anniversary, a celebration of thanksgiving was held at the IECLB's Mother Church, which through liturgy and preaching, revealed how the organization coordinates its thematic work. In most of the activities monitored, it is common for them to begin with a moment of reflection, from the perspective of the confessional tie (although always with an open perspective in ecumenical and inter-religious terms) of the organization.[73] This celebratory element is undoubtedly also part of the epistemology experienced by the organization, particularly with regard to the production of theological knowledge.

From the research process, it is possible to affirm that the production of theological knowledge about sexual and reproductive health and rights (SDSR) is not very clear in the organization (or its members). Although the central theological element for acting in this area is the concept of "transformative Diakonia," which underlies the work of the organization as a whole, a specific and clear articulation of this within SDSR was not identified. In general, they enter into the field of social activity that underlies the diaconal perspective that provides identity to the organization, but a theological foundation and a practical agenda in terms of articulation within the religious field could be expanded in order to widen and deepen

72. Participating at the Roundtable were Deacon Márcia Paixão, Daniel Souza (of the Ecumenical Youth Network), and Pastor Romi Bencke, Executive Secretary of the National Council of Christian Churches (CONIC).

73. At the meeting of the organization's team held on December 1, 2014, in which the team members participated, the initial meditation was on the topic of the HIV/AIDS epidemic from the viewpoint of a text from the Bible, and various issues related to health and sexual and reproductive rights were presented.

the work in this specific thematic area. To this end, the epistemological elements identified above (collective and participative production, use of the concept of Diakonia and its biblical-theological roots, continual education and training processes, networking and presence in various public and ecclesiastical spaces, and the celebratory element, among others) favor the possibility of these constructions.

In this sense, the approximation of the FLD to the Coletivo Feminino Plural also resulted in productive dialogue and articulations for knowledge production. That relationship is also a result of the research, particularly the PAR approach. The FLD's Small Projects announced in 2015 included a project about the dimensions of human rights, health, and sexual and reproductive rights, submitted by the Coletivo Feminino Plural. In addition, the two organizations monitored during the research developed joint activities at least at two other moments: Coffee with Sexual and Reproductive Rights[74] and in the aforementioned Seminar on Transformative Diakonia. Thus, it may be supposed that the research process fomented the reestablishment of a more solid dialogue between the two organizations. Thoughthey already had contact before, this research offered significant exchanges that have important epistemological implications relating to religion and theology with gender, feminism, and sexual and reproductive rights. This dialogue, and its results for both organizations also took shape because of the research project, particularly with regard to the use of the participatory research method.

Women'sGroup—Comunidade Floresta Imperial

In the Comunidade Floresta Imperial, two visits and seven meetings were held with a group brought together for this research. In both visits, the first to the pastor and the second to a meeting of the presbytery, the research project was developed with a group that had an interest in this discussion. Discussions were based on the demands and needs of the group itself, with respect to the community process as a whole.[75] The first contacts were es-

74. Coffee with Sexual and Reproductive Rights, promoted by FLD, occurred on August 26, 2015. During this activity, Télia Negrão, Coordinator of the Coletivo Feminino Plural, spoke on the history of sexual and reproductive rights, and the threats to these rights in the current context. André S. Musskopf, Coordinator of the research study, talked about approaching these topics in the field of theology, particularly within the scope of feminist theology, and a popular and feminist reading of the Bible.

75. At the first meeting with the pastor, the team members presented the research proposal and heard about the community's history and interests. The pastor then shared

tablished because there was a group in the community interested in discussing the topic of "homosexuality" because of some situations involving homosexual people within the community.[76] With the presbytery, it was decided that, at first, it would be important to be careful and to call people who had already expressed interest in discussing these issues. The invitations were made individually by the pastor, and the invited guests constituted a group of approximately eight women, aged between 40 and 80 years, who were active participants in the community. Some of these women had children who identified as homosexual. In fact, this was a theme that accompanied the discussions and reflections throughout the meetings. The meetings were also accompanied by the pastor and an intern.

The themes and methodologies used in each meeting were defined during the course of the meetings, having as a background the objective of the research and the questions raised by the participants. The first meeting, facilitated by Marli Brun[77] and Research Assistant Luciana Steffen, sought to sensitize the participants to the work to be carried out;they presented the research proposal and challenged the women to tell their personal stories, focusing especially on the issue of sexuality. Already in this first meeting, in which several group dynamics took place, the women shared narratives that helped in the construction of the plan for the activities that followed.

In the second meeting, after recalling the previous meeting, the participants were invited to talk about what they would like to discuss. The theme of homosexuality appeared strongly, often along with personal narratives concerning the subject. Many said they wanted to know more and understand the topic better to know how to deal with it. There was some discomfort, and even difficulty, in using certain words. The participants were then challenged to say what "is being said" or how people refer to homosexuals. At first, they were quite shy, but when provoked, they mentioned terms used to refer to homosexuals, and discussed the meanings. To provide visibility and record what was being said, words and phrases were recorded on brown paper placed on the floor in the center of the group.

the proposal with the presbytery, which invited the team to present the project. At the meeting with the presbytery, several questions related to the community context and the effects that this kind of discussion could have, as well as the best way to facilitate it, were discussed, considering all these issues. There was always interest in the activities.

76. Some of these situations were shared by the pastor as a way to understand the context of the community and were important to develop the activities with the group.

77. Marli Brun is Project Assistant for the Gender and Religion Program, a pastor of the IECLB, and has a Doctorate in Education.

There was little reference to theological/religious terms or issues, and when prompted to speak about them, many remained silent. The activity leaders avoided giving answers to the questions. Instead, they recorded and raised questions to be discussed by the group. The central question was, why is it so difficult to discuss sexuality in the context of the church? The meeting ended with the reading of two biblical narratives: on Jonathan and David and on Ruth and Naomi. The reading of the narratives was done with the names altered (so that they always reflected the relationship between a man and a woman). The participants were asked about the type of relationship that each narrative reflected.[78] Many were surprised to realize that the narratives referred to the relationship between two men and two women, respectively. This left the participants wondering what the correct narratives mean for the discussion of homosexuality in the Bible.

As it was a hot topic for the group, the next meeting dealt explicitly with homosexuality. It began with a cartoon that reflected on the impact of someone coming out as homosexual to their family. The cartoon features a neat dinner table, a man, a woman, and a hidden character who was asked what they wanted to be when they grew up. The answer: gay! Chaos ensues, the table is messed up, food and objects are thrown everywhere, the man is sick to his stomach, the woman tries to comfort him, and the character—a boy—is frightened and clings to the chair. The participants were invited to describe what they saw. In describing the story, they were commenting and reflecting on the situation and bringing up their own experiences or familiar examples that they were reminded of by the images. Next, they had to reflect on what would happen (or what happens) if someone "comes out" in the context of the church. They wondered what it would be like if it happened in the middle of a service. A drawing was made on paper, demonstrating a church service in the community and what would happen there if someone did "come out." At first, most said nothing would happen. In some sense, everybody would pretend nothing had happened, and the service would go on normally. The team suggested some possible reactions, such as some people getting up and leaving or mentioning biblical texts that supposedly condemn homosexuality. In general, the participants stated that they would try to treat the situation with discretion. For example, they would invite the person to talk somewhere else. They understood that

78. This exercise was proposed in Musskopf, "Bíblia, cura e homossexualidade," 100–103.

people might feel uncomfortable, but they would not necessarily take any specific action at that moment.

After this introduction, we talked about sexuality, starting with the questions "what is sexuality for?" and "why did God create sexuality?" Many of the questions regarding homosexuality revolved around this issue, especially when the subject of reproduction arose. An analogy was made with food, with questions about the participants' favorite food, why they like to eat some things and not others, how to eat, and where to eat, and so on. The act of eating, as something cultural, and involving affective memory and pleasure is not strictly "biological" or "natural." The group talked about sexuality as a gift from God and as a way of enjoying life, about themes such as contraceptives, condoms, and different forms of having and feeling pleasure. The aim was to understand that discussing homosexuality implies discussing sexuality in a broad way and that this topic concerns not only a specific group, but all people, and how they understand and live their sexuality. Once again, several stories and desires were shared. There was even an exchange of tips.

The following meeting sought to return to several of the issues raised throughout the previous meetings. The participants were invited to share how they felt in the meetings, what they reflected on, and how they felt about their experience. They felt more comfortable sharing their stories, doubts, and anxieties, but also their desires, joys, and pleasures. The main difficulty continued to be talking about those issues in relation to the Church and religion. Returning to some of the questions raised about how people refer to homosexuality in general and to homosexual people in particular, we suggested a reading of the narrative of Sodom and Gomorrah (Genesis 19).[79] When invited to say what they knew or remembered about the text, several had difficulty recounting the narrative, although some were aware of its association with the theme of homosexuality. After some fragments had been mentioned, the text was read, and a first conversation was held about it, its contents, and their impressions. Next, it was proposed to recount the narrative in their own words together and to construct a collective understanding of the text. The main highlight in the reading was the violence present in the text, which caused surprise when thinking about homosexuality and the homosexual people known to the participants. This exercise provoked other women's memories and narratives about their own

---

79. On the relationship between "sodomy" and homosexuality, see Jordan, *Invention*.

experience of sexuality, and how certain teachings construct a negative view of sexuality, perpetuating violent practices, especially toward women.

One of the recurring questions in the conversations, when one entered the field of religion and theology, was the reference to the narrative of creation and its use for condemning homosexuality (claiming, "God created man and woman"). To work on this theme, in the fifth meeting, the team prepared a very colorful table with fruit, flowers, and juices. Participants were invited to sit at the table and enjoy themselves. While they all ate and drank, they talked about the beauty and tidiness of the table, what each of them enjoyed the most, and especially the taste of food and drink. At one point, the first account of creation (Genesis 1) was read aloud, highlighting the creation of all things and the affirmation of the goodness of creation. Still at the table, the women had to write the names of a material object, a place, a person, and a body part they like on colored paper balls. The paper balls were next placed on a tree trunk drawn on paper on the wall, constituting a "tree of life." Then, unexpected situations were narrated that made the participants to relinquish each of the things they liked successively. Despite the different choices, the feeling of losing things that one likes and that somehow identify each person, provoked several reactions and reflections. The exercise sought to sensitize the participants. They discussed, in the following order, how many people lose material things or are prevented from being in places they like, people moving away and suffer violence that leaves marks on their bodies, because of the way they understand and live their sexuality, like homosexual people who lose their jobs, assets, friendships, and family relations, and suffer various forms of violence or are murdered for identifying themselves as homosexuals.

Next, the second account of creation was read (Genesis 2). Verse 7 was emphasized: "And the Lord God formed the human being from the dust of the ground and breathed into his nostrils the breath of life, and man became a living being." From this verse, a dynamic was proposed with balloons, in which the women were invited to fill the balloons with air, let the air come out gently, and feel it on their face, close it, and play with the inflated balloons filling the room, playing with them, forming pairs, and massaging each other with the balloons. Then, they were invited again to play with the balloons. At one point, they were invited to play with the blown-up balloons of the other participants. In the end, they all shared their ideas and feelings throughout the meeting, talked about how to care for others, and what challenges about sexuality the church faces in caring for people.

After this more "experiential" meeting, in the sixth meeting, it was understood that it was important to present some topics and information on the issues that were being discussed. Through a discussion and Pow-erPoint presentation (with information and images), we explored gender relations and language, to understand how our language is affected by a specific understanding about the different terms and concepts used to talk about homosexuality and sexual diversity (its history and meanings). We also discussed the difference between sex, gender, and sexuality. The participants asked questions and stated that they had never heard of most of these issues. An exercise was completed, involving reading the texts of the book of Leviticus (especially in relation to the term "abomination") to think about its meaning in the context in which it was used and how it could be read today. Finally, we talked about how the issues presented are dealt within the context of the church and the need for the community to be a safe space where we can talk about these issues and build care strategies so that people feel welcomed in their diversity.

In the last meeting, the team was surprised by the participants, who served a celebratory and farewell coffee. Before that, gathered in a circle as in the previous meetings, the trajectory of the meetings was reconstructed to remember what was done in each of them. As they recalled, the participants shared important issues and evaluated their experiences. Many used the word "liberation" to speak of the feeling they had after these experiences. They said that they felt freer to talk about these issues. Their relationships (including with their children) had changed. They felt that the topics studied, and how they were approached, were important to their lives and should be discussed with the whole community.[80] Many even felt challenged to think about how to work on these issues in the community, particularly what could be done to make the community a safe and welcoming place.[81]

As a final exercise, it was proposed to read two more biblical texts. Following the methodological steps used in other encounters, the women were first asked what they remembered about the text, then the text was read, and finally, the text was recounted and compared with other situations they were aware of. The first text was that of Matthew 8:5–13 (The healing of the

80. While systemizing the experiences, especially based on the photographic records, it was possible to perceive bodily changes in the women (the way they sat, the way they talked and presented themselves, and the way they would "get dressed" for the meetings).

81. One of the participants looked right at the pastor and asked, "What are you going to do about it?" A discussion followed about it being a task for all of them.

centurion's servant), paralleling the experience of homosexuals and other people who are not considered "worthy" in the church and in society. The text pointed to Jesus's unconditional welcoming and exaltation as "an example of faith." The second text was Luke 1:26–38 (Annunciation), as also discussed in other groups during the research. Here too, the women were surprised at the possibility of thinking of Mary in a new way: as the one with agency, who asks and decides in the dialogue with the angel Gabriel.

In the conversation about Mary, the question was raised as to how to speak about these matters in the church—what language is used and is available to speak about sexuality in religious-theological terms, and whether the participants understood themselves as producers of theological knowledge—particularly in relation to the work developed in the meetings.[82] From this conversation, a story shared during the meetings was explored; in which one of the participants shared an experience lived by her sister and her family. From this narrative, a prayer was formulated that was then shared with the women. It is the "prayer to Our Lady of the Deflowering Kettle":

> Our lady of the deflowering kettle,
> pray for us desiring and desirous women
> now and at the hour of the broken hymen. AMEN!
> Deliver us from the patriarchal coitus that invades us without lubrication,
> and from the slander of being considered impure and sinful.
> Fill us with the grace of orgasms of all kinds,
> When, how, and with whom we will.[83]

The women were asked if they identified with the prayer, if they imagined it could be used in community activities, and how they perceived it. Largely, the women reacted with surprise to the text, welcoming it as a form of joint theological production (research team and participants). The group gathered around the table, ate, drank, talked, exchanged hugs, thanks, took

82. One of the participants reported that on her sister's wedding night, her sister had been returned by the husband and his family, who alleged that she had not been a virgin when she got married. When the mother asked her about it, she reportedly said that one day when she was walking around the farm, the spout of a teakettle penetrated her vagina, and she bled. As the story goes, nobody put much faith in the girl's story, but it was accepted as "true," and the girl continued living with her husband. The story of the teakettle and the complicity of the other women saved her from community ostracism and other negativity that is a result of women who are considered "virgins who are no longer virgins."

83. The prayer was written by André S. Musskopf, after one of the encounters with the women's group.

photos, and committed to further discussion about sexual and reproductive health and rights.

The meetings with this group were all held in the community hall, next to the temple. They were affected by mutual trust-building through group interaction and, mainly, through the sharing stories. Many topics in the field of sexuality were discussed, and the participants felt free to share personal stories. Despite some shyness, there was also pleasure in sharing these stories, many of which the participants said they had never shared before. In other words, there was a lot of pain and suffering because of how these women's sexualities had been constructed; using their words, "that's how they taught us" or "no one ever talked about it like that."[84]

Another important element of the work with the women's group was the use of methodologies from popular education and the popular reading of the Bible. Some of the elements present started with their own experiences, gave voice to silenced stories, presented information and critical reflections, and built knowledge collectively from diverse knowledge. The use of biblical texts and narratives sought to bring reflections on theology and religion closer together and to encourage thinking about the place and role of the religious community in the production of bodies and sexualities. It is important to note that the participants felt less authorized to engage or to question values learned during the activities that involved working with biblical texts; many stated, "We do not know these things."

From the point of view of epistemology, the work conducted with the two organizations was fundamental to preparing the team for this last stage, both in terms of content and methodology. In this sense, the activities developed with the two organizations, those developed within the larger framework of the TSSRD Project, and the activities developed with the group of women in the community were intertwined in the reflection on the production of theological knowledge on gender and sexuality, pointing to theorizations and construction of practices.

Some Words by the Organizations and Groups

In the process of constructing this text, the last research phase was conducted. The final step was to return to the groups and organizations to discuss the results of the study. It is the return of the issues raised by the research and their discussion with the organizations and groups. This is an

---

84. This was also expressed in the desire to continue the reflection the following year: "The whole community should discuss these issues."

important step in the participatory research process, and it will certainly give rise to other elements that will be the object of future studies and reflections.

Nevertheless, before finalizing this text, it was understood that it was important to give voice to the subjects involved and to present some of their reflections on the process. To do so, the oral presentations were used as a source during the International Meeting on Theology and Sexual Health and Rights, which represented the formal closure of the project.

In his speech at the seminar, Rogério Aguiar, representing the Fundação Luterana de Diaconia, spoke about the organization's work and the challenges posed by the proposed research themes, on which the organization was already engaged. He also thanked the Gender and Religion Program (responsible for the implementation of the TSSRD Project) "for the valuable contribution of bringing to the FLD the themes (which we had already been discussing) related to sexuality and gender justice. Your intervention is very evident, and it greatly strengthened our work and our activities."[85]

Télia Negrão, speaking on behalf of the Coletivo Feminino Plural, began her speech stating, "For our organization, the Coletivo Feminino Plural, the partnership with the Gender and Religion Program of the Faculdades EST works almost like opening a window for a breath of fresh air. But this was a political construct that brought us deep reflections on the act of being a feminist."[86] She also spoke about the work developed by the organization and the current challenges regarding sexual and reproductive health and rights. She shared information and data about the Brazilian context, particularly regarding the role of religions.

About the challenge and the process triggered by the research, she said:

> Our decision was: we will open the doors and find out if we can build something in common, without prejudice, with an open heart. After two to three years, our hearts are more open, and I believe our spirits are more open. We found that among us, there were more women with beliefs and faith that we never could have imagined. . . some who do not believe and others who could not say it. We are discovering that in addition to religion, there is a realm of spirituality. It is necessary to explore this realm, and in this way, to create possibilities for new life experiences. . . . We have found in this work that feminist theology offers fundamental

85. Speech Aguiar, 2016.
86. Speech Negrão, 2015.

tools to understand the women with whom we work. While most Brazilian women say they have a faith or religion, many of them cannot say so, because they also have practices that are not in accordance with what the religions say is, right or wrong.[87]

Finally, she mentioned an activity organized by the Coletivo Feminino Plural, in commemoration of the organization's 20 years, for which Marcia Blasi[88] was invited as a panelist. Negrão reflected: "We were able to notice understandings and misunderstandings of the meanings religion can have. It is not something that oppresses, but which can liberate, help us to work from the heart, without the barriers and without the things that do not allow us to grow together."[89]

Resina Bohrz, pastor of the Comunidade Floresta Imperial, spoke on behalf of the women's group, mentioning the history of the community, the activities developed during the research, and the evaluation with the women after the research ended. About the meetings, she said: "The work was always very dynamic, involving the participants, making them feel very free and willing to talk about their lives. In the first place, you have to know yourself, your sexuality, and then understand the other person. This happened very spontaneously."[90] She mentioned the women's speeches in the evaluation process, saying:

> The study of the Biblical texts was very liberating for the participants. Especially for two of the women participants who have homosexual children, it was very important to participate in this group. They had the opportunity to speak openly about the subject, and this was extremely liberating. "It was like taking a weight off my shoulders," "I can now talk to my son, understand him better," said one participant. "It hurts inside to hear gibes from church people! We need to continue the reflection, but be careful about whom we choose to participate. There is a lot of prejudice!" said the other.[91]

---

87. Speech Negrão, 2015.

88. Marcia Blasi is a theologian and pastor who coordinates the Gender and Religion program of Faculdades EST.

89. Negrão, *Gênero e Saúde Mental.*

90. Speech Bohrz, 2016.

91. Speech Bohrz, 2016.

Final Reflections

It is difficult to measure and synthesize the lessons learned during the last three years within the framework of the research process. The methodological approach adopted—participatory research with popular education—undoubtedly provided opportunities for transformative experiences that escape systematization, but which are present in the individual and collective trajectories of the individuals, organizations, and groups that have been involved in this process. There is no denying that the choice of this methodological perspective allowed the production of knowledge with contributions to academic research, but also to practices already developed and to be constructed in different spaces.

In a sense, the research reaffirmed the theoretical and methodological tools of popular education and participatory research, Liberation Theologies, popular reading of the Bible, feminist, gender, and sexual diversity studies. However, fundamentally, the research affirms the importance of establishing and deepening relations and bridges between these theoretical and methodological perspectives, because when one enters the field of sexuality and sexual and reproductive rights, many of these ideologies still present conservative positions and do not allow themselves to be questioned by epistemologies that emerge precisely from experiences in the field of sexuality. As Marcella Althaus-Reid states, referring to queer theology, "it is in scenes of intimacy and the epistemology offered by those excluded from the heterosexual political project in theology that God's unveilings can occur."[92]

However, the research also reaffirmed the importance of connections between groups and networks in the production of knowledge. A resistance to deepening the theme of religion when working with the Coletivo Feminino Plural, a difficulty in finding a theological way to speak of the action in this field by the Fundação Luterana de Diaconia, and the difficulty for women in the Comunidade Floresta Imperial to feel empowered to speak theologically about matters of which they spoke relatively easily about when the relationship with the church and theology (or the Bible)[93] was not in question, reveal that these articulations, which can be facilitated by academia and research, are fundamental to finding new ways of speaking and acting in the field of sexual and reproductive rights. Theology and

92. Althaus-Reid, *Queer God*, 14.

93. In addition, many said that the problem was not the Bible or theology, but that "people are ignorant."

religion have a significant contribution to make. What we have seen in the development of this research was the importance of base groups, religious and social organizations, and universities working together in the production of theological knowledge about gender and sexuality.

This research has demonstrated that it is possible, and necessary, to produce theological knowledge not only *about* gender and sexuality, but also from experiences *within* gender and sexuality. Sometimes the difficulty seems to lie in finding a language that can articulate religious beliefs with sexual experiences. If, again, as Marcella Althaus-Reid says: "Theology is a sexual ideology performed in a sacralizing pattern: it is an orthodoxy (correct sexual dogma) and orthopraxis (correct sexual behavior), divinized sexually,"[94] then sexual narratives destabilize this ideology and seek other ways of saying this. They often do not fit into existing theological standards and models, create fissures, and implode these limited spaces of existence. New ways of doing theology are required, not only to legislate bodies and their relationships, but also to assume the ultimate materiality of bodies in relation and as the founding *locus* of theological doing; this will be an indecent theology.

94. Althaus-Reid, *From Feminist Theology to Indecent Theology*, 4.

Bibliography

Achutti, Luiz Eduardo Robinson. *Fotoetnografia: um estudo de antropologia visual sobre cotidiano, lixo e trabalho.* Porto Alegre: Tomo, Palmarinca, 1997.

Althaus-Reid, Marcella. *From Feminist Theology to Indecent Theology.* London: SCM, 2004.

———. *Indecent Theology.* London: Routledge, 2001.

———. *The Queer God.* London: Routledge, 2003.

"Comunidade Floresta Imperial completa 50 anos." http://portal.camaranh.rs.gov.br/noticias/3288.

Fundação Luterana de Diaconia. *Balanço Celebrativo FLD.* Caderno. Porto Alegre: FLD, 2015. http://www.fld.com.br/uploads/publicacoes/Balan%C3%A70%20Celebrativo%202015.pdf.

———. *Código de conduta.* Available at: http://www.fld.com.br/uploads/docinstitucionais/C%C3%B3digo%20de%20Conduta.pdf(last accessed June 23, 2017).

———. *Política de Justiça de Gênero.* Porto Alegre: FLD, 2014. http://www.fld.com.br/uploads/docinstitucionais/Pol%C3%ADtica%20de%20Justi%C3%A7a%20de%20G%C3%AAnero.pdf.

Gastellú-Camp, Adriana. *Como espiral de vida: aportes de la teologia feminista de liberación para otros modelos de liderazgo em las iglesias de América Latina y el caribe.* São Leopoldo: Faculdades EST/Instituto Sustentabilidade América Latina e Caribe, 2015.

Gebara, Ivone. "As epistemologias teológicas e suas consequências." In *Epistemologia, violência, sexualidade,* edited by Elaine Neuenfeldt et al., 31–50. São Leopoldo: Sinodal/EST, 2008.

Grupo Inclusivass. *Mulheres com deficiência: Direitos sexuais e direitos reprodutivos.* Porto Alegre, São Leopoldo: Grupo Inclusivass/Coletivo Feminino Plural, Programa de Gênero e Religião, 2016.

IECLB. *Constituição da IECLB.* http://www.luteranos.com.br/conteudo_organizacao/governanca-suporte-normativo/constituicao-da-ieclb-1.

Jara Holliday, Oscar. *A sistematização de experiências: prática e teoria para outros mundos possíveis.* Brasília: CONTAG, 2012.

Jordan, Mark D. *The Invention of Sodomy in Christian Theology.* Chicago: University of Chicago Press, 1997.

Josso, Marie-Christine. *Experiências de vida e formação.* São Paulo: Cortez, 2004.

Menezes, Marilu Nörnberg, ed. *Nem tão doce lar: uma vida semviolência—direito de mulheres e de homens.* São Leopoldo/Porto Alegre/Genebra: Sinodal/FLD/IECLB/LWF, 2012.

Menezes, Marilu Nörnberg. "Nem Tão Doce Lar." In *Ainda feminismo e gênero,* edited by André S. Musskopf and Marcia Blasi, 187–97. São Leopoldo: CEBI/PGR-EST, 2014.

Musskopf, André S. "Bíblia, cura e homossexualidade." *Revista de Interpretação Bíblica Latino-Americana* 49 (2004) 93–107.

———. *Via(da)gens teológicas: Itinerários para uma teologia queer no Brasil.* São Paulo: Fonte Editorial, 2012.

Musskopf, André S., et al. "Itinerários epistemológicos para uma pesquisa sobre saúde e direitos sexuais e reprodutivos no campo da teologia." *Coisas do Gênero* 1 (2015) 157–71.

Musskopf, André S. and Marcia Blasi edit. *Ainda feminismo e gênero.* São Leopoldo: CEBI/PGR-EST, 2014.

Negrão, Telia, et al. *Gênero e Saúde Mental: novas abordagens para uma linha de cuidado.* Porto Alegre: Coletivo Feminino Plural, 2015.

Oscar Jara e as fronteiras da extensão. http://www.ufrgs.br/prorext/news/oscar-jara-e-as-fronteiras-da-extensao.

Silva, Anelise Fróes da. "Mulheres em movimento (s): Estudo etnográfico sobre a inserção de feministas e lésbicas em movimentos sociais institucionalizados e autônomos nacidade de Porto Alegre/RS." PhD diss., UFSC, 2010.

Silva, Valéria Calvi Amaral. "Análise das relações entre quadros interpretativos e repertórios de ação em duas organizações feministas." PhD diss., UFRGS, 2013.

Steffen, Luciana. "Mulheres com deficiência, direitos sexuais e direitos reprodutivos: olhares a partir da Teologia." In *Anais do Simpósio Internacional da ABHR,* 474–75. Florianópolis: UFSC, 2016.

———. "Refletindo sobre Gênero, Deficiência e Sexualidade na Teologia." In *Anais do Congresso Internacional da Faculdades EST,* 3:43–50. São Leopoldo: EST, 2016.

Steffen, Luciana, and André S. Musskopf. "Direitos sexuais e direitos reprodutivos das pessoas com deficiências: implicações teológicas." *Revista Madrágora* 21 (2015) 39–65.

Steffen, Luciana, and Elisandra Carolina dos Santos. "As Inclusivass." *Coisas do Gênero* 1 (2015) 229–40.

———. "Direitos sexuais e direitos reprodutivos das mulheres com deficiência—Inclusivass." In *Anais do Congresso Latino-Americano de Gênero e Religião,* 4:508–24. São Leopoldo: EST, 2016.

3

Theology, Sexuality, and Christian Education

Towards an Inclusive and Liberating Christian Education

Remí Klein, Luciana Steffen

A boy, a young man afterward, and finally, a man, in whom, nevertheless, the boy continued to live. I was fascinated, in reading the Gospels, by the inseparability between their content and the method with which Christ communicated it. The teaching of Christ was not, nor could it be, that of one who, like many of us (thinking ourselves possessed of a truth), sought to impose or simply to transfer that truth. He Himself was the Truth, the Word made flesh, living history; His pedagogy was that of the witness of a Presence that contradicted, denounced, and announced. Incarnate Word, He Himself the Truth, the word that emanated from Him could not be a word that once said, was reported to have been, but a word that would always be. That word could never be learned if it was not apprehended and would not be apprehended if it were not equally "incarnated" by us. [. . .] His word is not sound that flies away: it is word with action. (Paulo Freire)[1]

Initial Considerations

The task of reflecting on the production of theological-pedagogical knowledge of health and rights, in the context of sexuality in the

1. Freire, "Conhecer, praticar, ensinar os Evangelhos," 7.

educational-religious process, breaks down several barriers, especially in the political and religious sphere. Issues such as gender, sexuality, and reproductive health and rights have often been addressed in a non-inclusive and non-liberating way. In this sense, Paulo Freire's epigraph on the pedagogy of Jesus challenges us in advance to exercise, in teaching and research, "the indivisibility between content and method" in Christian education, in the sense of "word/action."

This article presents the results of a research study on theology, sexuality, and Christian education, focusing on the educational-religious process, based on participatory research and research training, with a group of leaders from the Evangelical Church of Lutheran Confession in Brazil (IECLB). These leaders had been involved in developing teaching materials and initial and ongoing education for ecclesiastical-community action with children and adolescents. They focused especially on children's worship and confirmation teaching, with a specific emphasis on gender and sexuality issues.

This research was situated within a broader project entitled Theology, Sexual and Reproductive Health, and Rights(TSRHR),[2] developed by the Faculdades EST through the Gender and Religion Program, with the objective of researching and carrying out extension activities on theories and methodologies that enable education in sexuality and reproductive health and rights, within the scope of theological reflection and ecclesiastical practice in Latin America and the Caribbean. This was done from an interdisciplinary perspective, in dialogue with social and ecclesiastical organizations and groups, based on the principles of popular education and participatory research. The project, which ran from 2014 to 2016, was in partnership with the Church of Sweden and the Pontificia Universidad Javeriana of Colombia. In both educational institutions, individual research projects were conducted by the two specific research groups, and through exchange, cooperation, and joint activities.

---

2. This Project is a second phase of the Project, Theology and HIV/AIDS, conducted between 2010 and 2012, in four theological seminaries in Latin America, including the Faculdades EST, with the aim of teaching 28 masters' candidates, and conducting research related to the topic. At the evaluation seminar for this project, a second phase was proposed, through research, extension, and exchange, from a perspective of popular education and through participatory research. Thus, research projects in the area of sexuality and reproductive health and rights, in their interface with theology, were proposed.

Objectives and Research Methodology

Shared here are the main actions of the research, which aimed to investigate ways of producing knowledge about health and rights in the field of sexuality and human reproduction, in religious education contexts, i.e. in school and social action. This was based on epistemological and methodological references developed by Liberation Theologies and popular education, through joint participatory research and research training in Latin America, with contributions from feminist theology and gender studies. There was a view to producing a pedagogical and theological reflection on these topics and proposals for educational-religious action. The final product was a proposal for an inclusive and liberating Christian education, with particular attention to health and rights in the field of sexuality.

This research process unfolded together with bibliographical research and documentary analysis of educational benchmarks, both in the Brazilian public context and in the Lutheran Church, as well as in research training. This included autobiographical approaches that were descriptive, analytical, and robust, aiming at recalling, analyzing, and rethinking the educational-religious process, with particular attention to aspects of sexuality and sexual and reproductive health and rights. Attention was directed in this way in order to contribute to the systematization and the resignification of the state of knowledge on this topic in religious-educational communities. Community-specific approaches were geared toward Christian education in the Evangelical Church of Lutheran Confession in Brazil (IECLB), in its interface with religious teaching in schools, popular and human rights education in other social spaces in Brazil, as well as formal research, teaching, extension, and exchange outlets.

According to Gil, "Participatory research, like action research, is characterized by the interaction between researchers and members of the situations investigated. There are authors who use the two expressions as synonyms, as well as other labels."[3] In Latin America and the Spanish-speaking Caribbean, the term *participatory action research* (PAR) is well known, and the Colombian sociologist Orlando Fals is a renowned expert on this tool.[4]

From the perspective of the epistemological, pedagogical, and methodological importance of the research process, a participatory research process was employed. This is a concept that has been used since the 1980s in

3. Gil, *Como elaborar projetos de pesquisa*, 61.

4. As an example, see Fals, "La ciencia."

Brazil, especially as promoted by Carlos Rodrigues Brandão, in its interface with popular education. His research papers include *Pesquisa Participante* and *Repensando a Pesquisa Participante*,[5] and more recent works, such as *A Pergunta a Várias Mãos: A Experiência da Pesquisa no Trabalho do Educador*, and *Pesquisa Participante: O Saber da Partilha*, the latter of which was organized in partnership with Danilo Romeu Streck.[6] As Streck writes, "to research is to pronounce the world,"[7] thus intrinsically linking Freire's proposal with the method and methodology of participatory research.

In addition, there have been several studies related to the use of life histories and autobiographical approaches in teaching and research in Brazil, such as, for example, Maria Isabel Cunha,[8] Maria Helena Menna Barreto Abrahão,[9] and Elizeu Clementino de Souza[10] among others. Both Abrahão and Souza have referred to Marie-Christine Josso and her research-training proposal, with which they have established an interface for participatory research projects.

In addition to researching the sources in Marie-Christine Josso's[11] writings and her research-training proposal, we used research-related productions that interface between participatory research and research training, with a particular emphasis on the writings of Edla Eggert and Márcia Alves da Silva,[12] and the doctoral research of Marli Brun.[13] Based on the research training proposal, the authors perceive and conceive the process of inquiry as a "walk to oneself," and according to Marie-Christine Josso:

> The process of walking to oneself presents itself as a project to be built over the course of a lifetime, the conscious actualization of which passes, firstly, by the project of knowing who we are and what we think, do, value and desire in our relationships with others, and with the human and natural environment.[14]

5. Brandão, *Pesquisa participante*; Brandão, *Repensando a pesquisa participante*.

6. Brandão, *A pergunta a várias mãos*; Brandão and Streck, *Pesquisa participante*.

7. Streck, "Pesquisar é pronunciar o mundo."

8. Cunha, *O professor universitário*. One of the chapters deals specifically with narratives as producers and explainers of knowledge.

9. Abrahão, *A aventura (auto)biográfica*; Abrahão, *Tempos*; Abrahão, "Memoriais."

10. Souza, *O conhecimento*; Souza, *Autobiografias*; Souza, "A vida."

11. Josso, "História de vida e projeto"; Josso, *Experiências de vida e formação*; Josso, "A realização do ser humano como processo de transformação da consciência."

12. Eggert and Silva, "Observações sobre pesquisa."

13. Brun, *Bordando cidadania*.

14. Josso, *Experiências de vida e formação*, 59.

In this sense, Edla Eggert and Márcia Alves da Silva affirm:

> In this methodological perspective, it is a matter of perceiving the research process as part of a life trajectory of all those involved, plus the fact that the research process, in this perspective, can constitute an opportunity to reflect on its own course, from a perspective of projecting the future, both in the group and individually . . . From this methodological perspective, as well as in participatory research, there is a confluence between researcher and researched, since the researcher also feels involved in this process. In this methodology, there is no space for the discourse of neutrality and scientific objectivity, because, in this journey, everyone redraws their own trajectory.[15]

The project was approved by the Research Committee of the EST Postgraduate Council on November 26, 2014. It was also approved by the Commission of Experts of the Church of Sweden within the Theology, Sexual and Reproductive Health and Rights Project. Within the three-year research project, from 2014 to 2016, the related activities in 2014 were mainly writing and evaluation, bibliographic research, and an exploratory study on the theme and planning for activities in 2015, including the presentation of the project's studies on Theology and Sexuality, Reproductive Health, and Rights. In 2015, the work began with the research-training group, along with the continuation of the bibliographic research and analysis of Christian education documents and materials in the IECLB; the activities were completed in 2016.

Therefore, the first stage of the research project consisted of a bibliographical review and documentary analysis of curricular references and teaching materials, and a mapping of issues of gender, health, and sexual and reproductive rights, in their interface with religion and education. This was both at the level of public policies and ecclesiastical positions concerning the theme, with special emphasis on the Lutheran ecclesiastical sphere (IECLB). At that point, a documentary analysis was carried out in the Brazilian public educational context, regarding the incidence of policies on sexuality and gender issues in education proposals, and this was completed by the end of 2014. At the same time, bibliographical and documentary research was carried out in the Lutheran ecclesiastical context of the IECLB, with the purpose of reviewing the documents and analyzing religious, educational materials from the viewpoint of sexuality, health, and sexual and

15. Eggert and Silva, "Observações sobre," 51–68.

reproductive rights. The research project was concluded in 2016, with the support of the research training group.

In relation to the bibliographical research and documentary analysis of the references and teaching materials, mapping was carried out regarding the issues of gender, sexuality, health, and sexual and reproductive rights in their interface with religion and education. This was at the level of both public policies and the ecclesiastical positions concerning the topic, with special attention to the Brazilian Lutheran ecclesiastical scope of the IECLB. Thus, the research project became part of a broad field of theoretical references. A bibliographical review was proposed, with a mapping of the issues of gender, health, and sexual and reproductive rights in their interface with religion and education, based on the contributions of the theologies of liberation and popular education in Brazil and Latin America, together with feminist theology and gender studies.

Regarding the analysis of documents and teaching materials covering gender and sexuality in their theological-pedagogical interface with the educational-religious process, the IECLB Continuing Christian Education Plan(PECC)[16] was employed with the educational materials available from the coordinator of Christian education, who works on children's worship and adolescents' confirmation teaching. Thus, the latest volume of *Encontros Bíblicos com Crianças*[17] (*Biblical Encounters with Children*) and the new confirmation teaching material titled *Compartilha*[18] (*Share*) were used.

At the end of 2015, initial contacts were made for the third stage of the project. This part constituted a participatory research group that included research training for autobiographical reflection and analysison the educational-religious praxis related to the intersection with sexuality, health, and sexual and reproductive rights.

Previous procedures for the coordination of Christian education and the coordination of Gender, Generations, and Ethnicity of the General Secretariat of the IECLB were used. In agreement with both coordinators, ten IECLB leaders were invited to participate in the preparation of teaching materials, as well as the training for the ecclesiastical-community work

16. Igreja Evangélica de Confissão Luterana no Brasil, *Plano de Educação Cristã Contínua da IECLB (PECC)*; Conrad et al., *Educação comunitária*. We were members of the revision team for this material.

17. Witt, *Encontros Bíblicos com Crianças*. We were members of the team of revisers of the material.

18. Siegle, *Compartilha: Subsídio didático-1*; Siegle, *Compartilha: ensino confirmatório*.

with children and adolescents within the Church. Three members of these coordinating bodies, two teachers of Christian education in the theological training institutions of the Church, and five other representatives of five different Synods from three different states (Rio Grande do Sul, Santa Catarina, and Espírito Santo) were involved in the preparation of teaching materials. They were involved in the training of leaders in the area of Christian education for the work with children and adolescents, especially in children's worship and confirmation teaching. In addition, a teacher-researcher participated in the group; and there was direct and indirect support from the three other members of the TSSRD project team (coordinator and researcher, research assistant, and scientific initiation fellow). In the creation of the research training group, the proportionality of gender, age, training, experience, readiness, and availability for attendance at regular meetings held at the Faculdades EST during 2015 and 2016 were also considered.

The contacts were made, and the group was formed in early 2015. The group's first meeting was held in March 2015. Five meetings were held between 2015 and 2016[19] to study the reference documents and methodological combinations regarding the linking of participatory research with research training from the perspective of Christian education and gender studies, with autobiographical approaches ("self-writing"), based on the proposal of Marie-Christine Josso. The group also participated in the analysis of religious, educational materials within the scope of the IECLB, from the perspective of sexuality, health, and sexual and reproductive rights, as well as reflecting on possible proposals for an educational-religious initiative, with a view to an inclusive program andwith special attention given to health and rights in the field of sexuality.

In addition to the meetings, there was regular interaction through the opening of a virtual room on the Moodle platform of the Faculdades EST' website. In 2016, there was also an extension activity through the course on gender and Christian education at the Evaluation and Planning Meeting of the Synodic Department of Child Worship/Christian Infant Education, with the presence of children's worship coordinators from parishes of the Northern Santa Catarina Synod, assisted by Pastor Pamela Milbratz.

In 2016, the research report and meetings of the research training group were finalized, and the report was presented at the closing meeting of the *Theology and Sexuality, Reproductive Health, and Rights* projects in

---

19. Meetings of the group for the research training at Faculdades EST were held on August 27, 2015; October 15, 2015; March 3, 2016; June 16, 2016; and August 16, 2016.

Colombia[20] at the end of 2016. This was alongside the workshop, *Gender and Sexuality in Teaching Materials of the Church*, coordinated by the catechist MarianeNoely Bail da Cruz (the reference person of the research training group that participated in the event); the research assistant and Ph.D. candidate Luciana Steffen; and the scientific initiation scholar, the graduate student Raquel Wieland. The workshop socialized the results of the analysis of the IECLB teaching materials and the research training group's proposals for an inclusive and liberating Christian education.[21] The event brought together more than 250 people, including professors and researchers, religious leaders, representatives of civil society organizations, and organizations from Colombia, Brazil, Argentina, Sweden, and South Africa.

Results of the Bibliographical and Documentary Research

The Brazilian Educational Context

Regarding the bibliographic review and documentary analysis of the references and teaching materials proposed for the IECLB Christian education, including its interface with religious education, popular education, and human rights education, the research began with the policies on sexuality and gender issues in school education proposals. The extensive conference process at municipal, inter-municipal, state, and national levels culminated in 2014 with the approval and sanction of a new National Education Plan(PNE) following a lengthy process at the National Congress that did not incorporate gender or sexual orientation, among other issues included in the reference document. This illustrates the extent of the absence of sexual diversity in public education policies and the political and ecclesiastical

20. The communication titled *Gênero e Sexualidade na Educação Cristã*, prepared by Remí Klein and Laude Erandi Brandenburg, was presented by Professor Laude, representing the Research Coordinator, at the *Encontro Internacional Teologia, Saúde Sexual e Direitos*, which was held from November 29, 2016 to December 1, 2016 at the Pontificia Universidad Javeriana, in Colombia.

21. In terms of the presentation and publication of the texts about the research, there was also a communication titled *A importância do estudo de gênero e diversidad en a educação*, at the XV SICTI–Salão de Iniciação Científica, Tecnológica e de Inovação da Univates, in Lajeado/RS, by the scientific initiation fellow, Raquel Wieland. Likewise, the communication was published in the Annals of the Salão de Pesquisa da Faculdades EST: Wieland, "A importância."

pressure from both the Catholic Church and the evangelical wing of the National Congress and state and municipal legislative bodies.[22]

In order to draft a new PNE, originally planned for 2011–2020, the 2010 National Education Conference (CONAE 2010) was launched.[23] The final document resulted from the participation of members of the national educational community during 2009 and 2010. It was expected that the new 2011–2020 PNE would be prepared and approved, but this did not happen because of the delay in the proceedings in the National Congress on Public Law 8.035/10.[24] In 2013 and 2014, a new National Education Conference (CONAE 2014) was held, with municipal, inter-municipal, and state conferences. Thus, the PNE was approved only on June 25, 2014.

On the goals and strategies, it is worth noting that the 2014 document is the result of the CONAE 2010[25] deliberations. CONAE 2010's final document[26] addresses gender, sexuality, and rights in Axis VI, titled "Social justice, education, and work: Inclusion, diversity, and equality, highlighting the right to diversity and the need to overcome social, racial and gender inequalities":

> The issues of diversity, ethical and democratic treatment of differences, overcoming discriminatory and exclusionary pedagogical practices, and social justice apply to all institutions of basic and higher education, regardless of their nature and character.[27]

Also, on the issues of gender and sexual diversity, the CONAE 2010 final document lists 25 specific propositions, one of which is directly linked to the topic:

> g) Include studies of gender, gender identity, sexual orientation, sexual diversity, and sexual education, as a compulsory subject in the curriculum of initial and continuing education, in teaching, research and extension activities in undergraduate and postgraduate

22. As a specific result of this documentary analysis, an article was published in the magazine *Coisas do Gênero*, which presents more detail on the research: Klein, "Questões de gênero."

23. CONAE 2010, 15.

24. Brasil *Projeto de lei 8035/10.2010*. http://www2.camara.leg.br/atividade-legislativa /comissoes/comissoes-temporarias/especiais/54a-legislatura/pl8035-10-plano -nacional-de-educacao.

25. CONAE 2014, 10.

26. CONAE 2014.

27. CONAE 2010.

courses of study, in all areas of knowledge, in an interdisciplinary, transdisciplinary and transversal way, joining them together in the promotion of human rights, the goal of the National Human Rights Education Plan.[28]

The CONAE 2014 Reference Document had seven central axes and 519 propositions and strategies. Gender and sexuality issues were addressed in Axis II, titled "Education and diversity: social justice, inclusion, and human rights."[29] Among the 61 proposals and strategies of this axis, several dealt with gender issues, such as propositions and strategies 117, 118, 123, 125, 126, 131, 135, 139, 141, 142, 143, 145, 153, 155, 166, and 170. The term *diversity* prevailed, alongside other terms and expressions such as *disrespect, differences, discrimination, homophobia, gender identity, equality, intolerance, justice, lesbophobia, sexism,* the *feminist movement, sexual orientation, segregation, sexism,* and *transphobia.*[30]

The aforementioned propositions and strategies related to gender and sexuality are connected with issues of religion and education, for example, dealing with religious intolerance (proposition and strategy 117), as well as inclusion and human rights. This can be seen inproposition and strategy 119: "The issues of diversity, ethical and democratic treatment of differences, overcoming discriminatory and exclusionary pedagogical practices, are connected with the construction of social justice, inclusion, and human rights."[31]

In Strategy 5 of Axis II of the CONAE 2014 Final Document, we noted the following:

> To ensure, develop, and implement, in a collaborative manner, affirmative public policies at all levels, stages, and modalities, aimed at promoting ethnic and racial equality, disability, gender, and

---

28. CONAE 2010, 143–46.

29. CONAE 2013, 27–38.

30. CONAE 2013, 27–38.

31. CONAE 2013, 28; Klein, "Questões de gênero e sexualidade nos Planos de Educação," 148–49. As a participant at the CONAE municipal conference in São Leopoldo, Rio Grande do Sul, June 22–23, 2013, and a member of the Second Axis, we point out that in that axis, 25 amendments were voted on and approved. Several dealt with questions of gender, religious diversity, and religious intolerance; religious freedom and interreligious and intercultural identity, inclusion, and human rights education; and other aspects related to that axis.

human rights, and respect for religious diversity, through educational and social actions.[32]

The issues of diversity, gender, and sexuality are not restricted to Axis II, but rather pervade the entiredocument, as in the citation of the introduction of Axis I-PNE and the National System of Education, Organization, and Regulation:

> The consolidation of a SNE [Sistema Nacional de Educação–National Education System] that brings together the different levels and spheres of national education cannot be carried out without considering the principles mentioned, as well as the urgent need to overcome the social, ethnic-racial, gender and sexual diversity inequalities still present in society and at school.[33]

The Final Documents of both CONAE 2010 and CONAE 2014, explicitly and affirmatively, address gender and sexuality issues, but these issues were not the subject of the 2014–2024 PNE. Total omission and lack of clarification on these issues can be seen in the 20 strategies and actions proposed for the 2014–2024 decade. Only in general terms does Article 2 address these issues by referring to Section III of the PNE guidelines, which states, "overcoming educational inequalities, with an emphasis on promoting citizenship and eradicating all forms of discrimination."[34] The intervention of parliamentary and religious leaders to label gender issues erroneously as "gender ideology" was called into question. These issues were not incorporated into the PNE or subsequent state and municipal education plans.This became one of the most central and controversial subjects of its process at the national, state, and municipal levels.

The *National Curriculum Parameters*, developed and edited by the MEC [Ministério da Educação—Ministry of Education] in 1997, emphasized cross-cutting subjects or topics for the lives of citizens, among them cultural plurality and sexual orientation, stressing the importance of studying these subjects in schools.[35] In the public educational context, as a bibliographic reference, we highlighted the book *Sexual Education in the Classroom: Gender Relations, Sexual Orientation, and Ethnic-Racial*

---

32. CONAE 2014, 35.

33. CONAE 2014, 17.

34. CONAE 2014.

35. Brasil Secretaria de Educação Fundamental, *Parâmetros Curriculares Nacionais*.

Equality in A Proposal of Respect for Differences, by Jimena Furlani.[36] In the introduction to the work, Lourival José Martins Filho stated:

> the book reveals a fundamental commitment to teacher education for the construction of a Brazilian society that respects the sexual, gender, race and ethnic differences, religious worship, physical condition, class, origin, etc. . . . in an unequivocal alliance between political commitment, theory, and pedagogical practice. . . . curricula are not eternal, and neither are grids and chains. In addition, the internal dynamics of the school and classroom (and of society) may be different; the classroom has to be a learning space for children, adolescents, young people, and adults who dream of a world with other forms, colors, sounds, and touches because they are also children, adolescents and young people of different cultural identities.[37]

The Minister of Education, Janine Ribeiro, took a position on the controversy generated by the non-incorporation of gender and sexuality issues, asserting their inclusion in the curricular proposals of the schools, acknowledging that the Chamber of Deputies interfered by explicitly excluding issues of gender and sexual orientation from the text of the new PNE, and emphasizing that one of the goals of the PNE is "the eradication of all forms of discrimination."[38]

The National Education Council (CNE) also issued a public note on September 1, 2015, in which it states that it:

> is surprised—by the norms and guidelines in force—and concerned about educational plans that have been drawn up by Brazilian federal entities that have deliberately omitted the fundamentals, methodologies, and procedures regarding the treatment of the issues related to cultural diversity and gender, already duly enshrined in the normative *corpus* of Brazil for the construction of the citizenship of specific segments of the Brazilian population, and on which there can be no doubt as to the propriety of its treatment in the field of education. . . . In sum, the CNE considers that the absence or insufficiency of treatment of these singularities

---

36. Furlani, *Educação sexual.*

37. Martins Filho, "Apresentação," 11.

38. "National Education Plan of Brazil 2014," art. 3, para. III. http://pne.mec. gov.br/18-planos-subnacionais-de-educacao/543-plano-nacional-de-educacao-lei--n-13-005-2014.

means that the education plans that treated them are considered incomplete and should, therefore, be reviewed.[39]

Therefore, the groundwork has been laid for affirming the need for the revision and inclusion of gender and sexuality issues in education plans at different levels, as these are evident social themes that need to be approached from a human rights perspective, without considering gender as an "ideology," but rather as a cultural construction generating hierarchies, discrimination, and prejudice among people. That is why strengthening the guarantee of human rights and valuing diversity are fundamental to an inclusive and liberating education:

> From the analysis of the documents, more questions and doubts arise than conclusions and perspectives regarding the approach to these topics, with explicit crosscutting regarding influences and political and religious interferences in the field of education, especially in relation to gender and sexuality. At the same time, there are also explicit and encouraging indications on the part of the CNE and the MEC regarding the need to revise the plans that excluded such issues.[40]

Religious Context

After analyzing gender and sexuality issues in education, the bibliographical and documentary analysis of the teaching material is presented, especially considering the religious scope of the IECLB.

In ecclesiastical epistemological terms, the basic reference of the project is the document issued in 2013 by the International Department of the Church of Sweden entitled *Positioning on Sexual and Reproductive Health and Rights (SRHR).*[41] This document justifies the position of the Church of Sweden on SRHR and reads:

> Religions deal with a wide variety of everyday issues in the lives of individuals and communities. In various historical and cultural contexts, religious leaders and religious communities have

39. CNE, *Nota Pública.*

40. Klein, "Questões de Gênero,"154.

41. Igreja Da Suécia, *Posicionamento sobre Saúde e Direitos Sexuais e Reprodutivos (SDSR).* This is according to the Portuguese version of the document, translated by André S. Musskopf and available in the archives of the office of the president of Faculdades EST. Original text in English: Church of Sweden. *Position on Sexual and Reproductive Health and Rights (SRHR).* Policy Document. Uppsala: Church of Sweden, 2013.

exercised various levels of moral guidance or even control over the lives of individuals and communities. The ways in which religious texts are interpreted, and ideals and religious norms are formed, have an effect on how sexuality is understood. Because religious actors have social authority, they are in a position to legitimize and promote moral and social visions and to set standards on issues of sexuality and reproduction, and related issues of body and gender. Religious and cultural understandings significantly affect the ability of individuals to live an integral and satisfying life.[42]

The document states that this is more than a health issue and that

as a church, we have a special responsibility and a unique opportunity to work on issues related to sexual and reproductive health and rights . . .promoting a theologically empowering analysis of life to help improve the conditions for people to have the ability to live a life full of dignity, justice, and equality.[43]

In addition, in terms of other references for gender and religion, we must highlight the Lutheran World Federation'sdocument on gender justice policy, entitled *Towards a Common Path to Gender Justice: A Pedagogical Journey*, which states:

the pedagogical discussion on gender justice will contribute to a broader reflection on how we intend to teach, learn, follow, admonish and support each other as we continue to walk together, aiming at a communion in which inclusiveness is lived concretely.[44]

A document entitled *Gender Justice Policy* was also developed by Faculdades EST in 2015.[45] Accordingly, there are public and ecclesiastical benchmarks for the research project, which has a focus on Christian education from an inclusive epistemological and pedagogical perspective.

Thus, it is possible to consider the importance of gender and sexuality in a religious context. The bibliographical review and documentary analysis in the Lutheran ecclesiastical sphere regarding gender and sexuality aspects also included the IECLB Continuing Christian Education Plan (PECC), and the teaching materials currently available to coordinate Christian education for children and adolescents in worship and confirmation teaching.

---

42. Church of Sweden, *Position*, 2–3.

43. Church of Sweden, *Position*, 3.

44. Federação Luterana Mundial, *Política de Justiça de Gênero*, 2.

45. See also: Faculdades EST.

IECLB Continuing Christian Education Plan—PECC

According to the presentation by the Pastor President of the IECLB, the PECC "as well as being a planning tool, offers a theological and pedagogical framework for the educational process,"[46] aiming at "theologically and pedagogically guiding all instances of the IECLB in the evaluation, planning, and execution of Christian education initiatives for all phases of life, with a view to the better fulfillment of God's mission."[47]

The PECC, thus, provides guidelines for Christian education. In its text, there are several references to the importance of including gender and sexuality issues in Christian education. The PECC's theological foundation addresses the importance of studying gender and sexuality in relation to the following topics: the practice of love, dialogue, and respect as an expression of unity, baptism, justification by grace and faith, and Christian freedom. It also features texts about dialogue, respect for diversity, plurality, social justice, love, and non-discrimination. In the PECC's pedagogical foundation, the pedagogical action of Jesus Christ as based on life experience (John 4:1–30) and overcoming prejudices (Mark 5:25–34)[48] emphasizes the importance of acting against prejudices around gender issues and sexuality. The methodological initiative includes topics such as "valuing people's life experience," "involving the whole body," and "humanizing education through joy."

As in the subject areas, the PECC emphasizes the importance of hermeneutics and exegesis in biblical reading, as well as the consideration of contexts involving questions about gender and sexuality: "it is imperative that the Christian education actions proposed in all instances of the IECLB contemplate the study of themes that pervade personal and community life in the social, political, economic, cultural and religious contexts."[49] Another section states:

> Postmodern society has peculiar cultural traits. Cultural diversity is increasingly explicit in the globalized world. However, gender, race, ethnicity, religion, sexual orientation, and even language have been used as a basis for excluding people. [. . .] This: This multicultural society demands of the Christian faith a constant exercise of love and tolerance in the face of diversity. Furthermore, it calls

46. Friedrich, "Apresentação," 5.
47. IECLB, *Plano*, 13.
48. IECLB, *Plano*, 21.
49. IECLB, *Plano*, 37.

for a deep commitment to the incarnate gospel, which opposes all situations that oppress and hinder the freedom of the people.[50]

The PECC affirms the inclusion of gender and sexuality issues in Christian education, and the following presuppositions are mentioned: love of neighbors, non-discrimination, justice, dignity, and respect for diversity and plurality. Thus, this document, a theological and pedagogical reference for the IECLB, justifies the study of these themes in Christian education.

Analysis of the Teaching Materials

The analysis of teaching material included the last volume of *Encontros Bíblicos com Crianças (Biblical Encounters with Children)* and new material for teaching confirmation, *Share*. The materials were analyzed with the help of the research training group and other participants in the project, such as the research assistant and the scientific initiation fellow, with the objective of analyzing the IECLB teaching materials regarding their approach to gender and sexuality issues in the educational-religious process, especially for children and adolescents.

Share

The book *Share* consists of two volumes, each of which includes a text for confirmation class students and others for lesson guides. It contributes to confirmation teaching in the IECLB, for youth ages 11–13. It includes questions about gender diversity and respect and equality, as well as inclusive language, alongside the representation of diverse races and ethnic groups and the inclusion of people with disabilities. Both the texts and illustrations highlight these issues. The books sometimes contain very complex, difficult-to-interpret texts. Also, in many IECLB communities, confirmation teaching is conducted by laypeople, who complicate the understanding of theological terms used in the material.

The books could also do more to explore gender issues. The texts that cover the issues of gender in volume 1 of *Share* are included under "Gender in the Context of Confirmation Teaching,"[51] where the author, Marcia Blasi, writes:

50. IECLB, *Plano,* 38.
51. Blasi, *Apresentação.*

84

Gender as a category of social analysis refers to social, cultural, and theological constructs used to define what it is to be a man and what it means to be a woman in a given context, defining what is valued, expected and allowed for men and women . . . It is very important in working with adolescents, to keep the subject in mind at all meetings. Gender is not a matter for women and girls, but rather for all people. In all activities, one must beware of generalizations and prejudice . . . Proposing discussions in this area is very salutary and necessary and is part of the process of growing in faith.

Marcia Blasi uses accessible language to describe the tasks expected of different genders. She explains that colors and toys should not be differentiated by gender, and neither should the division of tasks. These should be assigned in accordance with each person's abilities, not by gender.[52] Providing texts that include gender and sexuality issues for counselors, as well as for children and adolescents, is crucial for their reflection on gender discrimination in diverse spaces, including within their own homes, in relation to the division of domestic tasks or domestic violence.

In addition, in Volume 1 of the lesson guide, the lesson "Image and Likeness of God" states, "Every person is unique and important to God. He accepts us as we are, regardless of gender, ethnicity, physical characteristics, or social position." In the same book and in that for the confirmation class students of both sexes is the topic "We Have Differences," which states that each person is unique, and that God made all people in His image and likeness, equal in value and dignity.[53]

In the guidebook, the topic "How is your family?" offers the following highlight:

The different situations lead to rethinking the family model and what constitutes the family in its essence. Women have conquered public space and the labor market; children participate in family decisions; jobs are shared. As defined by the United Nations, the family requires at least two interrelated members for kinship, adoption, or marriage relationships. This means that the concept of a family exceeds the limit of residence, and its members can live in different places without ceasing to be a family . . . With the changes that the family has suffered over time, it becomes difficult to speak of families linked much more by affection than by social

---

52. Wieland, A importância, 25.
53. Siegle, Compartilha: Subsídio didático, 1:30; 42; 44.

convention. Such affectivity includes values, such as respect, understanding, trust, dialogue, and care.[54]

The guidebook, Volume 2, contains a lesson called "The Community
of Jesus" that singles out certain women in the Bible who followed Jesus:

> Probably, there were still other people whose names we do not
> know. By the names quoted, we realized that the group around Je-
> sus was not only composed of men. Women played a very impor-
> tant role in all of Jesus' activities. Women were the first witnesses
> of the resurrection.[55]

In the book for confirmation class students, the lesson "Ecumenism:
The Search for Unity" states, "We live with people who think and act differently than we do. This diversity of actions and thoughts helps us to look at
the world from other perspectives . . . Living with diversity requires openness and respect."[56]

Thus, in *Share*, gender-related topics are evident; however, for issues
of sexuality, there are no specific questions about respect for diversity alone.

Biblical Encounters with Children

Volume 4 of *Encontros Bíblicos com Crianças* (*Biblical Encounters with Children*), intended for children attending children's worship at the IECLB, also
contains questions about gender. Inclusive language is present, and several
biblical stories with women are mentioned, giving them visibility and affirming their dignity. Only in one of the stories (Judges 4 and 5), Deborah
is not valued, but the text seems to imply that everything that happens in
the narrative is to God's credit, alone.[57] John 20:1–18 also values Mary, the
first to encounter the resurrected Jesus. Thus, as Siegle has written, "Jesus
Christ calls all people, regardless of gender, and invites us to stand on the
way, going to meet people, and living the Passover."[58]

The text about the Samaritan woman (John 4:1–42; Genesis 21:9–21)
mentions that Jesus treated her well, but it does not contest the injustice nor
discrimination besetting the Samaritan woman because she was married

54. Siegle, *Compartilha: Subsídio didático*, 1:67.

55. Siegle, *Compartilha: Subsídio didático*, 2:27.

56. Siegle, *Compartilha: Subsídio didático*, 2:89.

57. Siegle, *Compartilha: Subsídio didático*, 2:38.

58. Siegle, *Compartilha: Subsídio didático*, 2:59.

several times and is seen as sinful and unworthy.[59] Likewise, the text of Genesis 21:9–21 comments on the sexual relationship between master and slave and polygamy, accepted at the time. The slave became pregnant and was sent away and was looked after by God.[60] The message centers on the mother figure, on Mother's Day, and reinforces the myth of the zealous mother, by saying that God is like a caring mother who is always attentive. Yet, the approach does not problematize the slave's situation.

Some stories are about marriage, but the messages have a different focus and do not problematize marriage. One text is about domestic chores in an all-male family; a re-assigning of tasks often assigned to women (Matthew 21:28–32) and deconstructing gender roles. There are also biblical texts that address equality between people, demonstrating how each person is loved and received by God as part of His creation (James 2:1–10), as well as the importance of not distinguishing or discriminating between different people.[61]

Thus, in the book, *Biblical Encounters with Children*, there are texts that highlight the value of women, while others do not. There are texts that propose to deconstruct gender roles, but others that reinforce them. The subject of sexuality appears in some ways, but overall it is ignored and not problematized. The focus of the message is elsewhere, especially in the stories about polygamy and a woman who is excluded because she has been married more than once. The texts on equality mention that all people should be accepted and respected, but nonetheless understood as independent of their gender and sexuality.

Research Training Group and Extension Activity

The research-training group had five meetings. The first meeting (August 27, 2015) focused on group interaction, familiarization with the project, and study of reference documents and methodological combinations regarding the linking of participatory research with research training in the perspective of Christian education and studies, with autobiographical approaches ("self-writing"), based on the proposal of Marie-Christine Josso. At the second meeting (October 15, 2015), the study of methodological references continued, and the first three in-person "self-writing" sessions began; they had already been shared in the virtual room. There was also

---

59. Siegle, *Compartilha: Subsídio didático*, 2:44.

60. Siegle, *Compartilha: Subsídio didático*, 2:89.

61. Siegle, *Compartilha: Subsídio didático*, 2:51; 92.

a study of the text "Observations on autobiographical research from the perspective of popular education in Gender Studies,"[62] and a presentation by research assistant Luciana Steffen on positioning in sexual and reproductive health and rights (SRHR).[63] This was followed by a debate on the concepts of sexual and reproductive health, sexual and reproductive rights, and their links with gender and sexuality issues.

The topics were: 1. Rights to sexual and reproductive health as fundamental to human experience and social relations; 2. the Church of Sweden promoting universal access to understandable sex education; 3. the Church of Sweden promoting universal access to health care services; 4. the Church of Sweden's commitment to a respectful and mutual dialogue on the religious and cultural understanding of sexuality and sexual and reproductive health, with the aim of supporting a positive understanding of sexuality and a common commitment to respect, protection, and fulfillment of health rights and sexual and reproductive health for all; 5. the Church of Sweden opposing cultural and religious practices and norms that are harmful to the integrity of an individual's body; and 6. the Church of Sweden recognizing that there is a connection between power, sexuality, and reproduction.[64]

Reports and reference materials were also posted in the discussion forum, allowing the group to interact outside of physical meeting spaces, on the Faculdades EST website, through postings and discussions about materials and their self-writings. The two meetings had seven and then six members, respectfully. In addition to justified absences, there were two withdrawals due to changes in labor regulations and work-related conflicts.

The research training group met three times in 2016 (March 3, June 14, and August 16). The March 3 meeting was followed by the self-writing meeting. The June 14 meeting included the last two group self-writing sessions and the beginning of the joint analysis of IECLB materials (the PECC, *Biblical Encounters*, and *Share*), as well as the preparation of proposals for educational-religious action with a view to developing inclusive and liberating Christian education, with particular attention to sexual health and rights.

At the last meeting, on August 16, the group finalized the systematization of proposals from the previous meetings' discussions, including reflections from self-writings on experiences involving children and adolescents

62. Eggert and Silva, "Observações."

63. Church of Sweden, *Position*.

64. Church of Sweden, *Position*.

in the IECLB, the experience of developing the teaching materials and the PECC, as well as personal experiences around gender and sexuality. We also investigated the "Creative Communities Seminar-Cross-cutting Themes for Christian Educationand Pedagogical and Methodological Principles for Christian Education"to determine whatthey contained on gender, sexual and reproductive health, and sexual and reproductive rights.

This seminar was carried out within the framework of the IECLB communities, with a view to training and motivating leaders involved in Christian education work with children, adolescents, young people, and adults in the IECLB, addressing the theological and pedagogical foundations of Christian education for all phases of life through the PECC. The seminar also considered issues of gender and inclusion as transversal themes in Christian education and conducted practical workshops based on theater, music, and plastic arts, relating theoretical reflection to practice. The seminar was organized by the coordinator of Christian education of the Training Secretariat of the IECLB, which is responsible for the publication of materials and training for the IECLB leaders. Training courses for leaders are offered in partnership with the Synods, especially for people in charge of working with children, adolescents, and young people. In this sense, the "Creative Communities Seminar" has been an in-service IECLB training course in this area of Christian education.

The seminar addressed gender issues, as opposed to sexuality, in particular. Gender issues were present in the seminar's proposal, while issues related to sexuality, corporeity, and sexual and reproductive health and rights were not explicitly addressed. The materials used in the seminar explain the importance of cross-cutting themes such as gender and that this theme is not only about women, but also about everyone helping to rethink reality and transform it. The difference between gender and sex is explained, in that gender is a social, non-biological construction that refers to the social gender roles that men and women are expected to perform, where male and female people are educated to be men and women, respectively, within a given context or reality. The materials also emphasize the generalizations, prejudice, and discrimination provoked by gender roles, as well as the notion that the division of tasks must be carried out according to the abilities of each person and not of their gender, as well as the importance of inclusive language and care, with a balance between women and men in the images and examples that leaders use in communities. It was also suggested that gender issues be addressed during commemorative dates. Finally, the materials stress that everybody has the same rights and must be respected in their differences.

At the last meeting, the group also pushed to organize and hold a seminar for training IECLB leaders who prepare teaching materials and are involved in initial and continued training for ecclesiastical-community action involving children and adolescents, according to the specific objectives of the research project. The goal was to propose an educational-religious initiative for inclusive and liberating Christian education, with a specific focus on health and rights in the field of sexuality for a training seminar at the IECLB. Thus, the research-training group decided which training seminar to feature and proposed the topics to address, including gender roles, inclusive language, gender and power, corporeity and puberty, sexuality, biblical texts that encompass themes, new family models, and sexual abuse using the documentary *The Beginning of Life.*[65]

The International Meeting on Theology and Sexual Health and Rights was held in November 2016, at the Pontificia Universidad Javeriana in Colombia, to close the research project. A representative from the research-training group was invited to present on the group and report their experiences, and to run a workshop presenting the research results. At the end of the meeting, the work of the research training group was evaluated; thus, concluding its activities.

Seven to eight people participated in the five meetings of the group, and in one meeting, one person participated virtually by Skype. Regular members of the TSSRD project team and a research fellow sat in on the meetings.

Parallel to self-writing, the research training group was motivated to participate in an extension course called "Gender issues in community life: A challenge for all people," conducted by the Sustainability Institute, to continue their training on gender and sexuality issues. The course lasted ten hours in the virtual environment provided by Faculdades EST. It was self-instructional and free of charge.[66] Thus, the group collectively formed a proposal in this area, using a theological, pedagogical, and methodological approach, with a historical panorama and conceptual explanations referring to the theme of gender and sexuality issues, and with educational challenges for the churches. The group discussed experiences of the extension

---

65. Direction and production by Estella Renner.

66. See http://www.est.edu.br/extensao/cursos/visualiza/questoes-de-genero-na-vida-comunitaria-.

course, considering it a relevant learning experience. The way gender issues were posed went far beyond inclusive language, stressing, and affirming the importance of fundamental gender issues. This discussion was also important in thinking about proposals for an inclusive and liberating Christian education, as will be discussed below.

The Writings of the Self

Beginning with the motivational text of Marie-Christine Josso and with the project's epistemological and methodological references, the challenge was for each participant to write about and share, both online and in the face-to-face meetings, a narrative about their formative experiences in Christian education. This was from both a personal (in terms of their educational-religious process) and professional (in terms of leadership training andteaching materials) perspective, at the interface of theology, sexuality, and Christian education, focusing on the research project. A passage from the "Poem to the Oralist," by José Carlos Sebe Bom Meihy[67] was recited to motivate and invite participants' self-writing:

> Lend me your voice . . . Give me the word, which is yours, the right to be me; let me tell you how it was, as I see it, or at least as I saw it . . . I have a story, mine, small, but unique. Ask me anything you want, but let me tell you how I feel . . . Lend me what I need: the voice, the letter, and the book to say that I have experienced life and that, in spite of everything, I am also history.

In this sense, we attempted to recover daily life and invisible life histories, in a narrative and reflexive way, in relation to the educational-religious process at the interface of gender and sexuality, self-examining one's own stories. Also serving as inspiration were Jorge Larrosa's words:

> Tell yourself your own story . . . Remember your future and walk until your childhood. And do not ask who you are to the one who knows the answer, not even to that part of you that knows the answer, because the answer could kill the intensity of the question and what stirs in that intensity. Ask yourself the question.[68]

From this existential and pedagogical perspective, the research-training group recalled their own stories, not as nostalgia or idealization

---

67. Meihy, *(Re)introduzindo história oral no Brasil*, vii.
68. Larrosa, *Pedagogia profana*, 41.

of the past but to achieve "the nexus of social reminiscence in becoming."[69]
According to Paul Ricœur:

> our own existence cannot be separated from the way in which we
> can realize ourselves. It is in telling our own stories that we give
> ourselves an identity. We recognize ourselves in the stories we tell
> about ourselves.[70]

This process gradually occurred in a climate of trust, freedom, and
confidence among the members, effectively constituting a research-training
group. Some questions about gender and sexuality are highlighted below, as
determined by the analysis of the members' self-writing.

One example of the writing stressed issues surrounding adolescence
during confirmation teaching, with clumsy bodies chasing after a soccer
ball on the churchyard, and the timidity of the body in the dynamics of
hugs and touches. Happiness and fear of losing the title of "virgin mouth"[71]
were also clear. Nonetheless, some issues were evident at the confirmation
retreats, which lasted a whole week. Girls menstruating for the first time
asked what to do. For boys who had homosexual tendencies, related questions were included and monitored.[72] The effervescence of adolescent
sexuality was evident in confirmation teaching, as well as the explicit difficulty of dealing with corporeity, gender, and sexuality issues during the
educational-religious process.

Another member's report expressed themes of sexuality and gender
by recounting a woman becoming pregnant before marriage and the ensu-
ing religious interactions; they addressed the feelings of guilt and rejection
by families and society. This self-writing narrated her mother's pregnancy,
describing how the author's father took responsibility for the pregnancy.
Her mother, nonetheless, assumed the guilt and responsibility for becoming pregnant before marriage, which was a disappointment to the paternal
grandfather, who wanted his son to enjoy life more before having a family
and blamed the mother for ruining his life. Thus, during childhood, the
grandfather often gave the author's mother "disapproving glances" when

---

69. Larrosa, *Pedagogia profana*, 79.

70. Ricœur in Larrosa, *Pedagogia profana*, 41.

71. "Escrita de si" by a member of the group on research training, shared at the meeting on March 3, 2016.

72. "Escrita de si" by a member of the group on research training, shared at the meeting on June 14, 2016.

they passed in the street. So, she hid her crying. This child was considered the "fruit" of her parents' sin.[73]

One self-writing referenced sexual abuse by relatives during child-hood, which caused trauma, guilt, and psychosomatic effects. One of the relatives would threaten to hurtthe child's father, in order to guilt the child into obedience. Moreover, in this self-writing, the group member had the role of welcoming the church community, as a manifestation of God's love and care. At Sunday school, as a child, she felt loved by God and was sure that He would always be there to take care of her.

In that same report, the member also expressed her thanks to God for helping her spouse to think differently than her father and for having a friend, who was also a Christian educator, who demonstrated that she could study and be whomever she wanted. She could even get married and have a child, without needing to depend on her father or spouse to tell her what to do, especially when deciding what is best for herself and for the people she loves, and for improving her life. She mentioned that her life-history was affected by the things that men can do and women cannot, by the things that women must do, and men do not, and by the freedoms that men have and the ways in which women are bound. These were always part of her life and have restrained her speech and thoughts as part of the "chains of sexism" that have long been instilled in both women and men.[74]

It follows that experiences shape feelings and attitudes throughout life. Learning from others' experiences, however, can help people, especially women and girls who face similar situations. Thus, members of the group through their reportscan understand some of what other girls and women have gone through, obtain support and comfort, and recover from hurt. One participant also pointed out that experiences in the faith community helped them to turn their life around and that God enables us to build anew.[75]

One long and intense piece of self-writing, shared in confidence with the research-training group, described maternal feelings of rejection and guilt over premarital pregnancy, as well as family and social experiences of sexism and harassment. It also shared gestures of friendship, trust, and

73. "Escrita de si" by a member of the group on research training, shared at the meeting on March 3, 2016.

74. "Escrita de si" by a member of the group on research training, shared at the meeting on March 3, 2016.

75. "Escrita de si" by a member of the group on research training, shared at the meeting on March 3, 2016.

acceptance in marriage and in the religious community. Above all, it included an expression of faith in divine love and unconditional acceptance as a motivation for a just and liberating Christian education, especially in relation to women.

Another self-writing discussed gender and sexuality, describing how the author never felt limitations or stigma for being female, and how sexuality was presented much later in her life, but not very clearly. As a result of her time and education at home and in church, she was raised with the idea of a "natural" family, as the school taught, which would be a white family, with a father, mother, and two or three children.[76]

Thus, through the self-writings, gender and sexuality issues appeared to have affected people's lives, sometimes through negative experiences. This finding affirms the importance of working on these issues in an inclusive and liberating manner.

Creative Communities Seminar

The IECLB Training Seminar, organized by the North-Catarinense Synod, included a proposal for an educational-religious initiative to develop inclusive and liberating Christian education and with special attention to sexual health and rights. It was held on August 27 and 28, 2016, at the Vila Elsa, in São Bento do Sul, SC, at the Evaluation and Planning Meeting of the Synod's Department of the Children's Worship/Christian Education, with the participation of counselors who coordinate the Synod's children worship. These meetings have been held since 1998, with the objective of forming parish leaders, sharing experiences, and strengthening these people for their work in the church. The topics of gender and sexuality were important themes in previous meetings.

The research-training group, with the endorsement of the coordinator and research team of the Theology, Sexuality, and Christian Education Research Project, proposed training on these topics with the assistance of Pastor Pamela Milbratz. The training included Christian education, sexuality, gender justice, diversity, and the family through dynamic readings of biblical texts and analyses of the documentary, *The Beginning of Life*, produced by Estela Renner. The scientific initiation scholar, graduate student Raquel Wieland, followed the activities.

---

76. "Escrita de si" by a member of the group on research training, shared at the meeting on June 14, 2016.

Proposals

Based on the bibliographical and documentary analyses that included gender and sexuality issues in politics and religion, in particular, the analysis of the IECLB teaching materials and the research training group's self-writings, the group reflected on and systematized the proposals for educational-religious action with a view to developing inclusive and liberating Christian education that focused on gender and sexuality issues. Thus, as a proposal, the group affirmed the importance of work on gender justice, gender roles, women's visibility, inclusive language, and respect for different forms of family, which had already appeared in some materials and documents; however, more in-depth, regularly updated materials are required on these topics.

However, sexuality, sexual and reproductive health and rights were practically absent from the analyzed teaching materials. The group suggested that this absence should be addressed. Some specific themes proposed for work with children were body care, privacy, the right to choose, sexual abuse, appreciation and respect for the body, and differently abled bodies. For adolescents, the group suggested teaching about issues of sexuality, changes in the body, sexual violence, preventing the spread of sexually transmitted diseases, contraceptive methods, and abortion.

These topics should be addressed using both teaching materials and training courses. The group emphasized the importance of teaching materials (primers) for families and Christian education leaders, addressing how to guide children (as well as adolescents, adults, and older people) with regard to the body and sexuality. Material that is more systematic is necessary to serve as a basis for reflection, in line with the foundations of the Church, as concluded by the PECC, which supports studies on gender and sexuality.

Face-to-face courses in these topics for ministers, students of theology, members of the Church, and community leaders in Christian education are fundamental, and printed materials resulting from the discussions in these courses must be made available for others' consultation. Based on the analysis and positive evaluation of the distance-learning extension course mentioned above, *Gender Issues in Community Life: A Challenge for all People*,[77] other distance learning courses have also been proposed (In Brazil this is called "Educação a Distância"—EAD), such as a course that includes

77. Seehttp://www.est.edu.br/extensao/cursos/visualiza/questoes-de-genero-na-vida-comunitaria-.

both gender and sexuality, with the support of the IECLB's coordinating bodies. In addition to gender issues, which were presented in an illustrative and practical way, it was also proposed to include questions about sexuality. The texts in the distance-learning course can also be included in books, booklets, and other materials.

As presented in Volume 2 of *Share*, it is important to propose retreats for adolescents in which they can learn about gender, their bodies, and sexuality issues. Nevertheless, these terms presented conceptual difficulties. Many people in the communities do not participate in activities with themes of gender and sexuality. Thus, it was proposed to start with the themes of gender and the body, and then, to move onto the more delicate subjects that might cause embarrassment and rejection.

Final Considerations

In summary, corporeity, gender justice, and inclusiveness were the keywords that emerged during this research. The general goal and specific objectives of the research project were achieved, despite the resistance to gender and sexuality issues in the educational process, whether in the family or church, excerpts from the self-writings, or the analysis of the IECLB teaching materials.

During the research process with the training group, the theme of corporeitywas evident more than the theme of sexuality. The research included more gender issues than questions about sexual and reproductive health and rights. Because of the absence of sexuality-related themes in the documents and teaching materials, the group predominantly raised questions about the body and gender. However, gender is a theme in sexual and reproductive health and rights, which involve non-discrimination based on gender, sexual orientation, or sexual behavior, among others. Conversations about gender support the principle that all rights must be guaranteed for all people, regardless of gender identity.[78]

Sexuality and gender are still considered taboo themes and are not usually treated explicitly; instead, they are seen as invisible and designated as "gender ideology," even more so when it comes to issues of homosexuality and feminist theology. However, the Freirean presupposition of the place and role of education in general, and of Christian education in particular, is

78. IPPF, *Direitos Sexuais.*

part of social transformation: "If education alone does not transform society, without it neither does society change."[79]

The PECC offers important input for the study of gender and sexuality in Christian education, emphasizing love for our neighbor, non-discrimination, justice, dignity, respect for diversity and plurality, and the importance of considering different contexts and realities. It is also important to emphasize the words of Pastor Marcia Blasi again, in the analysis of the teaching material *Share*. She stresses that it is very important to consider gender in all encounters when working with adolescents because this is a theme for all people. We must be careful with generalizations and prejudices. The discussion in this area is then beneficial, necessary, and part of the process of growth in faith.[80]

Thus, in proposals for an inclusive and liberating Christian education, the following research themes are fundamental for the educational-religious processes for children and adolescents in the Church: gender, sexuality, health, and rights. However, these themes, especially sexuality, are absent from the teaching materials and training courses. This research, therefore, highlights the need for further attention to this area.

This research into theology, sexuality, and Christian educationalso uncovered reminiscences[81] of how people came to be who they are and how they constituted their identity as people and educators."[82] We conclude by paraphrasing Almir Sater's *Tocando em Frente*: "Each of us composes their story and each being, in themselves, carries the gift of being capable of being happy."[83]

79. Freire, *Pedagogia da indignação*, 67.
80. Blasi, *Apresentação*, 9–10.
81. Klein, "Reminiscências escolares," 105–13.
82. Larrosa, *Pedagogia profana*, 181.
83. Sater and Teixeira, *Tocando em frente.*

Bibliography

Abrahão, Maria Helena Menna Barreto, ed. *A aventura (auto)biográfica—Teoria and Empiria*. Porto Alegre: Edipucrs, 2004.

———. *Tempos, narrativas e ficções: a invenção de si*. Edipucrs. Porto Alegre, 2006.

———. "Memoriais, memória, trajetórias docentes e formação continuada de professores: a invenção de si em seminário de investigação-formação." In *Trajetórias e processos de ensinar e aprender: didática e formação de professores* edited by Edla Eggert, 448–86. Porto Alegre: Edipucrs, 2008.

BÍBLIA SAGRADA. Antigo e Novo Testamento. Tradução em português por João Ferreira de Almeida. Ed. rev. e atualizada no Brasil. Brasília, DF: Sociedade Bíblica do Brasil, 1969.

Blasi, Marcia. *Apresentação*. In *Compartilha: ensino confirmatório—uso do confirmando e da confirmanda*, edited by Carmen Michel Siegle, 9–10. São Leopoldo: Sinodal; Porto Alegre: IECLB, 2014.

Brandão, Carlos Rodrigues. *A pergunta a várias mãos—a experiência da pesquisa no trabalho do educador*. São Paulo: Cortez, 2003.

———. *Pesquisa participante*. São Paulo, SP: Brasiliense, 1984.

———. *Repensando a pesquisa participante*. São Paulo, SP: Brasiliense, 1984.

Brandão, Carlos Rodrigues, and Sreck, Danilo Romeu, ed. *Pesquisa participante: o saber da partilha*. Aparecida: Ideias e Letras, 2006.

Brasil Secretaria de Educação Fundamental. *Parâmetros Curriculares Nacionais: Pluralidade Cultural, Orientação Sexual*. Brasília: MEC/SEF, 1997.

Brun, Marli. *Bordando cidadania: projetos de conhecimento de mulheres na preservação do Wandschoner em Ivoti (2007–2013)*. PhD diss., UNISINOS, 2013.

Church of Sweden. *Position on Sexual and Reproductive Health and Rights (SRHR)*. Uppsala: Church of Sweden, 2013.

CNE. *Nota Pública às Assembleias Legislativas, à Câmara Legislativa do DF, às Câmaras de Vereadores, aos Conselhos Estaduais, Distrital e Municipais de Educação e à Sociedade Brasileira*. http://www.cnte.org.br/index.php/comunicacao/noticias/15472-nota-publica-as-assembleias-legislativas-a-camara-legislativa-do-df-as-camaras-de-vereadores-aos-conselhos-estaduais-distrital-e-municipais-de-educacao-e-a-sociedade-brasileira.htm.

CONAE. Conferência Nacional de Educação 2010. *Documento Final*. http://conae.mec.gov.br/images/stories/pdf/pdf/doc_base_documento_final.pdf.

———. Conferência Nacional de Educação 2013. *Documento referência*. http://conae2014.mec.gov.br/images/pdf/doc_referencia.pdf.

———. Conferência Nacional de Educação 2014. *Documento final*. http://conae2014.mec.gov.br/images/doc/Sistematizacao/DocumentoFinal29012015.pdf.

Conrad, Débora Raquel Klesener, Ponick, Edosn and Voigt, Emílio, ed. *Educação comunitária*. Manual de estudos. Série Educação Cristã Contínua. São Leopoldo: Sinodal, 2011.

Cunha, Maria Isabel. *O professor universitário na transição de paradigmas*. Araraquara, SP: J. M. Editores, 1998.

Eggert, Edla. *Educa-teologiza-ção: fragmentos de um discurso teológico (mulheres em busca de visibilidade através da narrativa transcrita)*. Dissertation, Escola Superior de Teologia, 1998.

Eggert, Edla, and Silva, Marcia Alves da, ed. *A tecelagem como metáfora das pedagogias docentes*. Pelotas: UFPel, 2009.

———. "Observações sobre pesquisa autobiográfica na perspectiva da Educação Popular nos Estudos de Gênero." *Contexto and Educação* 26 (2011) 85, 51–68.

Faculdades EST. *Política de justiça de gênero*. http://www.est.edu.br/ouvidoria/template/docs/Politica_Justica_de_Genero-final.pdf.

Fals, Orlando. "La ciência y el Pueblo: nuevas reflexiones sobre la investigación-acción." *La sociología en Colombia: balance y perspectivas. Memoria del Tercer Congreso Nacional de Sociología*, edited by Asosación Colombiana de Sociología, 149–74. Bogotá, 20 a 22 de ago, 1980.

Federação Luterana Mundial. *Política de Justiça de Gênero*. Genebra, Suíça, 2014. Text edited by Elaine Neuenfeldt and translated to Portuguese for the IECLB by Luís Marcos Sander.

Fórum Nacional de Educação. *CONAE 2014: Conferência Nacional de Educação: documento—referência*. Brasília: Ministério da Educação, 2013.

Freire, Paulo. *À sombra desta mangueira*. São Paulo: Olho D´Água, 1995.

———. "Conhecer, praticar, ensinar os Evangelhos." *Tempo e Presença* 154, 1979.

———. *Pedagogia da indignação: cartas pedagógicas e outros escritos*. São Paulo: Editora UNESP, 2000.

Freire, Paulo, and Guimarães, Sérgio. *Aprendendo com a própria história I*. Rio de Janeiro: Paz e Terra, 1987.

———. *Aprendendo com a própria história II*. Rio de Janeiro: Paz e Terra, 2000.

Friedrich, Nestor Paulo. "Apresentação." In *Plano de Educação Cristã Contínua da IECLB (PECC)*, edited by Igreja Evangélica de Confissão Luterana no Brasil, 5. São Leopoldo: Sinodal; Porto Alegre: IECLB, 2011.

Furlani, Jimena. *Educação sexual na sala de aula: relações de gênero, orientação sexual e igualdade étnico-racial numa proposta de respeito às diferenças*. Belo Horizonte: Autêntica, 2011.

Gil, Antonio Carlos. *Como elaborar projetos de pesquisa*. 3rd ed. São Paulo: Atlas, 1991.

Josso, Marie-Christine. "A realização do ser humano como processo de transformação da consciência: ensinar, acompanhar e aprender: um mesmo desafio para uma vida em ligação." In *Trajetórias e processos de ensinar e aprender: práticas e didáticas*, edited by Edla Eggert et. al., 17–58. XIV ENDIPE. Livro 02. Porto Alegre: Edipucrs, 2008.

———. *Experiências de vida e formação*. São Paulo: Cortez, 2004.

———. "História de vida e projeto: a história de vida como projeto e as 'histórias de vida' a serviço de projetos." *Educação e Pesquisa*, São Paulo 25 (1999) 11–23.

Igreja Evangélica de Confissão Luterana no Brasil. *Plano de Educação Cristã Contínua da IECLB (PECC)*. São Leopoldo: Sinodal; Porto Alegre: IECLB, 2011.

IPPF. *Direitos Sexuais: Uma Declaração da IPPF*. Rio de Janeiro: BEMFAM, 2009. http://www.apf.pt/sites/default/files/media/2015/direitos_sexuais_ippf.pdf.

Klein, Remí. *Histórias em jogo: rememorando e ressignificando o processo educativo religioso sob um olhar etnocartográfico*. PhD diss., Escola Superior de Teologia, 2004.

———. "Processo educativo-religioso: histórias 'em jogo' e novos olhares 'em formação." In *Formação de professores: abordagens contemporâneas*, edited by Selenir Kronbauer and Margareth Simionato, 71–89. São Paulo: Paulinas, 2008.

———. "Questões de gênero e sexualidade nos Planos de Educação." *Coisas do gênero* 1 (2015) 145–56.

————. "Reminiscências escolares." In *Tempos de escola: memórias*, edited by Beatriz T. Daudt Fischer, 3:105–13. São Leopoldo: Oikos; Brasília: Liber Livro, 2012.

Larrosa, Jorge. *Pedagogia profana: danças, piruetas e mascaradas*. 4th ed. Belo Horizonte, MG: Autêntica, 2004.

Martins Filho, Lourival José. "Apresentação." In *Educação sexual na sala de aula: relações de gênero, orientação sexual e igualdade étnico-racial numa proposta de respeito às diferenças*, edited by Jimena Furlani, 67. Belo Horizonte: Autêntica, 2011.

Meihy, José Carlos Sebe Bom, ed. *(Re)introduzindo história oral no Brasil*. São Paulo: Xamã, 1996.

Menezes, Marilu Nörnberg, ed. *Nem tão doce lar: uma vida sem violência—direitos de mulheres e de homens*. São Leopoldo; Porto Alegre; Genebra: Sinodal; FLD; IECLB; LWF, 2012.

Sater, Almir, and Teixeira, Renato. *Tocando em frente*. MPB [s. d.].

Siegle, Carmen Michel, ed. *Compartilha: ensino confirmatório—uso do confirmando e da confirmanda*. São Leopoldo: Sinodal; Porto Alegre: IECLB, 2014.

————. *Compartilha: Subsídio didático para o Ensino Confirmatório: Livro de Orientação—1*. São Leopoldo: Sinodal; Porto Alegre: IECLB, 2014.

————. *Compartilha: Subsídio didático para o Ensino Confirmatório: Livro de Orientação—2*. São Leopoldo: Sinodal; Porto Alegre: IECLB, 2015.

Souza, Elizeu Clementino de. "A vida com as histórias de vida: apontamentos sobre pesquisa e formação." In *Trajetórias e processos de ensinar e aprender: didática e formação de professores*, edited by Edla Eggert et. at., 135–54. XIV ENDIPE. Livro 01. Porto Alegre: Edipucrs, 2008.

————, ed. *Autobiografias, histórias de vida e formação: ensino e pesquisa*. Porto Alegre: Edipucrs; Salvador: Eduneb, 2006B.

————. *O conhecimento de si—estágio e narrativas de formação de professores*. Rio de Janeiro: DP&A; Salvador: Uneb, 2006A.

Streck, Danilo Romeu. "Pesquisar é pronunciar o mundo: notas sobre método e metodologia." In *Pesquisa participante: o saber da partilha*, edited by Carlos Rodrigues Brandão and Danilo Romeu Streck. Aparecida: Ideias e Letras, 2006.

Wieland, Raquel. "A importância do estudo de gênero e diversidade na educação cristã." In conference proceedings *Salão de Pesquisa da Faculdades EST*. São Leopoldo, 2016.

Witt, Maria Dirlane, ed. *Encontros Bíblicos com Crianças, Volume 4*. São Leopoldo: Sinodal, 2014.

4

HIV and Spirituality

An Update on their Interconnection[1]

Introduction

Since its appearance in the 1980s, the reality of HIV has been an undeniable fact.[2] Today, thanks to advances in medicine, HIV/AIDS is recognized in

1. This research was developed under the responsibility of the research group, "Teología y mundo contemporáneo" (Theology and the Modern World), at the School of Theology of the Pontificia Universidad Javeriana and was sponsored by the Church of Sweden, which issued a call along the lines of what it wanted to support 2014–2016: "Theology and Sexuality and reproductive health and human rights." The research was developed by Silvia Susana Becerra, Nelson Mafla, Olga Consuelo Vélez, Adriana Hoyos, Andrea García, María Clara Castro, and Elsa Cristina Morales. The collaborators were Elisa Bautista and Angela Rivas. The research was accompanied by master's students David Lima and José Leonardo Rincón. We are grateful to the patients who supported the research: Gabriel Beltrán, Carlos González, Henry Prieto, and Myriam Rodríguez. Thanks also to Professors Salvador Rincón and Lorena Duarte for their collaboration in the Yoga and Theater sessions of Psychophysical Gymnastics. Finally, we are grateful to the volunteer students who supported the research in various ways: Leidy Johana Gamba, Diana Pinzón, Ana María Montes, Paula Melissa Rosa, Gina Carranza, Camila Velasco, Ehimy Mateus, and Daniela León. Author details: Olga Consuelo Vélez Caro, Theologian with a master's degree in Theology from the Pontificia Universidad Católica of Rio de Janeiro, full professor and researcher at the School of Theology of the Pontificia Universidad Javeriana, coordinator of the research group, "Theology and the Modern World," at the Facultad de Teología de la Pontificia Universidad Javeriana, ORCID code: 0000.0002-4663-8005, email ocvelez@javeriana.edu.co; Silvia Susana Becerra Melo, master's degrees in theology and socioeconomic planning, sbecerra@javeriana.edu.co; Nelson Mafla Terán, Doctor of Sciences in Religion, Nelson.mafla@javeriana.edu.co; Adriana Hoyos Camacho, holder of a master's degree in Theology, aahoyos@javeriana.edu.co; María Clara Castro Arango, nurse, mccasara@husi.org.co; Elsa Cristina Morales, social worker, ecmorales@husi.org.co; Luz Ángela Rivas, artist and art therapy teacher, lalarivas30@gmail.com; David Lima, S.J., Theology graduate, dlima@javeriana.edu.co; Salvador Rincón Arcila, master's degree in Yoga, s-rincon@javeriana.du.co; Elisa Bautista, undergraduate student of religious studies, Elisa_bc10@hotmail.com; Andrea García Becerra, agarcia@javeriana.edu.co.

2. The first cases in Colombia were detected in 1981. See Ministerio de Salud y

the Western world as a chronic disease, which means that it is no longer considered a fatal disease, and many patients have undetectable levels of the virus and enjoy their quality of life. Although there has been progress in understanding this disease, its transmission, and its control, much work remains to be done as stigma and discrimination toward people living with HIV/AIDS (PLWHA) still exists. In addition, the comprehensive care required to keep the virus sufficiently under control to enjoy a quality of life pervades the economic, social, personal, and affective spheres. The treatments require an economic perspective because they are costly, and health care organizations to which patients are affiliated are not always able to subsidize the treatments.

Moreover, many patients do not have an affiliation with a health organization. The treatments require a social perspective because stigma and discrimination affect the acceptance of adequate treatment; it may seem better to hide the disease, so as not to forfeit social acceptance. The treatments require a personal perspective because there are so many medications, sometimes with adverse side effects, that PLWHA need to have personal discipline and continuous adherence to the prescribed treatments. In addition, treatments require an affective perspective because people are an integral part of the comprehensive care. Health, affection, and spirituality go hand in hand. People who love themselves nourish their spirituality, forgive their mistakes, seek to improve themselves and even more, feel loved, strengthened, accepted, and connected during difficult trials in their lives and are more capable of maintaining meaning in their lives; this keeps them stable and happy. However, when this does not happen, sadness, depression, loneliness, and rejection win.

Among the many perspectives that can be investigated with respect to HIV, we wanted to study the way PLWHA relate their spirituality to the conception they have of their corporeity and sexuality. This relationship was chosen because the body and sex are intrinsic to understanding the disease, and because in the experience of believers, body and sex have been misunderstood categories. They have often been considered as something inferior to the spiritual, or even the cause of sin. However, throughout history, there have been various attempts to overcome these negative

---

Protección Social República de Colombia, *Panorama del VIH-SIDA en Colombia, 1983–2010. Un análisis de situación*, 19. However, according to the latest research, it dates to the late nineteenth century (1884–1924), not 1939, as had been believed. For further detail see: http://www.elmundo.es/elmundosalud/2008/10/01/hepatitissida/1222879761.html.

conceptions. At present, there is much more openness to viewing them in a more integrated and positive way.

The aim, therefore, is to demonstrate how the understanding of these two realities—corporeality and sexuality—have different nuances in their affirmation as theological places, where the revelation of God happens through saving and exercising mercy. To achieve this objective, Participatory Action Research (PAR)[3] was employed, focusing on a group of PLWHA who were cared for within the infectious diseases unit at the San Ignacio University Hospital. There, relevant data was collected, and conclusions were made.

The theological perspective used was based on the same divine revelation evident in duly interpreted history, in "deeds and words,"[4] making it possible to reveal the presence of God where it seems it could not occur but, contrary to what one might think, revealing more clearly the divine design of human history as a shared fate.

This is what Carmiña Navia argues by referring to the reality of the new emergent minorities (such as indigenous people, Afros, women), but that we could also apply to PLWHA: "These new places allow us to visualize with deep respect the religious experience of those who are beyond the limits. And that experience will then become the source of a revelation that will demonstrate other possibilities for the Divine face, whose radiance is hidden if it is enclosed in languages or in symbols that have stopped communicating."[5]

This research article consists of four parts. In the first section, we refer to the methodology. In the second section, we present the theoretical framework that supported the research and allowed us to understand the data. The third section is a presentation of the data and its interpretation. Finally, the conclusions and pastoral guidelines that follow from the research carried out are proposed.

---

3. This method requires beginning with the interlocutors, with whom the needs are determined, and knowledge is built in a transforming way, through tools that allow the collective construction of knowledge among the different actors, in order to achieve social transformation. See: López de Ceballos, *Un método*.

4. *Dei Verbum*, 2. https://www.vatican.va/archive/hist_councils/ii_vatican_council/documents/vat-ii_const_19651118_dei-verbum_en.html.

5. Navia, "Nuevos discursos."

Methodological Assumptions

The starting point that guarantees the development of scientific knowledge is the method, and from this, we begin by presenting PAR,[6] which guided this investigation. All science is specified by its method, and this is how theology, understood as a "mediation between a certain cultural matrix and the meaning and function of a religion within the said matrix,"[7] necessarily refers us to methodology. The reason for this affirmation is that if theology conceives of culture in its classical meaning,[8] there is not much need to think about its method because its objective is to reflect on its nature, and it is considered a completed accomplishment that is transmitted from generation to generation and repeated as formulated. However, when theology is conceived as a mediation between culture and religion, where culture is "the set of meanings and values that inform a certain way of life," and religion is religious pluralism, then theology is a developing process, always underway. Its guarantee of a rigorous foundation depends on its methodology.

Thus, we begin to consider theology as a mediating discipline between the facts of reality and the revelation of God in the facts. In other words, we assume a way of conducting inductive, contextual, situated theology, imbued with contemporary challenges, and with the explicit desire to respond to them. Within such a paradigm, PAR is very well suited.

General Characteristics

With a long history in Latin America, PAR is a typical method of the social sciences and aims to produce knowledge and transform the researched reality. We used it for this reason, as we are aware of the decades-long debate regarding Liberation Theology and the use of social mediation. We are also aware that the primacy of theological work is faith, but we believe that to assume this method in order to approach reality offers the possibility

---

6. For a more detailed presentation of this method and its articulation with the theological method see: Vélez, "El que acer teológico."

7. Lonergan, *Método en Teología*, 9.

8. By classical culture, Lonergan understands one single culture that is universal and permanent. Its norms and ideals may be the object of the aspirations of uneducated people, and "empirical" culture is understood as the set of meanings and values that inform a certain way of life. It may remain unchanging for centuries, or it may also be submitted to a process of slow development or rapid disintegration. Cf. Lonergan, *Método en teología*, 9.

of grasping it sufficiently. And, from this, it offers reflections from faith. Logically, this first approach is made from faith, because individuals who study theology and assume a method do not act in a neutral way. Rather, everything they are and believe affects their study of theology. This is how the PAR method is used by believers and non-believers; but, recognizing the starting point, they allow themselves to question the facts of reality and to remain aware of the "autonomy of earthly reality" (*Gaudium et spes* 36), seeking to offer a reflection in the light of faith.

However, what is the Participatory Action Research (PAR) method? This method emerged as "an intentional way to empower people, so that they can take effective action towards the improvement of their living conditions. The novel thing is not that people question their conditions and look for better ways to act for their well-being and that of their community, but the fact of calling this process research and conducting it as an intellectual activity."[9]

PAR is a methodology that combines theory and praxis. It is considered "a cyclical process of action-reflection-action."[10] It is characterized by breaking down the barriers between the individual who investigates and the objects that are investigated. It proposes that the subjects and objects of the reality to be investigated constitute themselves as subjects/researchers, thus promoting a horizontal relationship among all of the participants. It is true that researchers (who could be called academic or specialized) often approach a situation and propose in that context to carry out research involving contextual participants. However, the challenge they have, when proposing the PAR methodology, is to be able to act as "facilitators," seeking to empower the participants to become researchers of their own reality.

PAR starts from the assumption that the social sciences are not neutral, but that their intellectual manifestations affect the material and symbolic life of societies. In the same way, it assumes that researchers also have their own postulates as social subjects, and from there, they carry out their research. That is to say, all knowledge has its "pretexts" or "intentionalities," and the "from where" which necessarily orients the researcher's task.

PAR raises questions about the methodological, operational, and technical procedures of traditional research, and is an essential conceptual and methodological resource to produce knowledge and the transformation of reality in Latin America. Subsequently, it is not a methodology with

9. Park, "Qué es la investigación-acción participativa," 137.
10. Kirchner, "La Investigación Acción Participativa (IAP)," 2.

a single template.[11] Different authors[12] can be identified in their particular contexts, and this has produced PAR with different templates.

PAR implies a new epistemological, methodological, ethical, and political approach.[13] Epistemological because it supposes breaking down the classic positivist separation between the subject and object of investigation. In this case, the subjects are the object of their own knowledge, and this implies that truth is achieved in participatory community action. It is methodological because it assumes that everyone participates in a procedural manner in the structural knowledge of reality, with the aim of transforming it. The qualitative, participative methods and the collective construction of the results are privileged. It is ethical because this attitude is necessary to work with human groups in the solution of their problems. In itself, PAR is an ethical position vis-à-vis the researched communities: it is an attitude towards knowledge and facing the participating actors. There is a condition of equality between the academic researcher and all participants, which generates a different attitudinal and axiological context compared to other types of research. Finally, it is political because it implies the transformation of reality by generating knowledge that is a new attitude towards power.

In other words, "lived experience" acquires a fundamental role in the construction of knowledge. Here it is not about investigations "out there," but about "human existences" carrying their own problems and the urgent need to transform them.

Many other features of PAR exist; however, what interests us is presenting how it was used in this investigation, and the following section addresses this.

Research Ethics

This research is the result of research withPLWHA, a population that has been affected by various forms of stigma and discrimination. Subsequently, the following ethical requirements have been taken into account:

- Informed consent form: with the support of the hospital and the patients, this document was prepared and presented at three meetings,

11. Leal, "La Investigación Acción Participación," 14.

12. Some meaningful authors: Latin American: Freire, Bosco, Cohen, Fals, Mariño, Vio, Cendales, De Sousa. United Kingdom: Elliott, O'Haniòn. Australia: Mc Taggar, Gruñid. See: Leal, "La Investigación Acción Participación," 21.

13. See García Sánchez and Barón, *Núcleos de Educación Social*, 88–89. Kirchner, "La Investigación Acción Participativa (IAP)," 3.

in which interested parties were invited to participate. The goals of the research were presented, together with the methodology that was going to be used, the people and institutions involved, and the problem that was to be addressed. The patients were listened to, and following their suggestions and comments, some adjustments were made to the objectives, and the problem posed.

- The will of the patients: it was emphatically stated that no one was obliged to participate and that if the participants did not want to participate or if during the process they wanted to withdraw, they were free to do so, and this would have no impact on the service that the hospital was offering them. It was made clear that the photos, videos, interviews, and their contributions in the investigation were strictly confidential. These materials would be used only by virtue of the investigation. In the case of the interviews, the names would be changed to maintain the patients' confidentiality. Once they were clear about the process and had agreed to it, they signed the informed consent form.

- Benefit for the population of PLWHA: likewise, we confirmed that the results obtained in the process would be based on the welfare of PLWHA, which implies that the results will be returned not only to the hospital but also to the patients, who will be able to dispose of them without limitations.

Finally, as researchers, we set out to determine the most appropriate language and the best means to carry out empathetic, respectful, and non-invasive work, where we not only share knowledge but also respect life. We were called upon to humanize ourselves through these realities, to analyze the research in-depth, and assume a reflection that contributes to the transformation of an inclusive spirituality, free of stigma.

Subject Population, Techniques Used, and the Results

To conduct the research, a team was formed that composed of health professionals from the Infectious Diseases Unit of the San Ignacio University Hospital, patients, theologians, students in the Master of Theology program, and student volunteers from the area. It was a plural, diverse, and interdisciplinary team for understanding and thinking about the research.

With the team formed, the research question was rethought, in such a way that it responded to the interests of all the participants involved. The research tools and techniques that would most help accomplish the goal of the investigation were sought, and the roles and responsibilities were agreed. The process was lived out in an atmosphere of trust and closeness, which allowed us to maintain a sensitive and compact team that experienced many lessons and transformations. It was an experience that touched our souls, and it is challenging to translate this into words.

The research partners were patients assigned to the Infectious Diseases Unit of the San Ignacio University Hospital (HUSI), which serves about 1700 PLWHA, who visit for monthly consultations and medical check-ups. With this population, three prior meetings were held to share the research proposal, listen to their contributions, and define the objective, tools, and most appropriate means for conducting the investigation jointly. Throughout the three years, various techniques were used to obtain the data and analyze them, as described below.

Survey

Only 123 surveys were completed (a little less than 10 percent of the patients attended the HUSI) as there was resistance from some patients, and others did not attend the meetings proposed for the exercise, because, as noted, PLWHA fear stigmatization and prefer to remain anonymous.

The questions collected quantitative data, but from them, we could infer reflections that will be discussed in Section 3 of this article. The survey included 39 questions to gather general data, such as gender, age, education, economic position, family support, sexuality, and relationship with God, among other issues. Of the 123 respondents, 114 were men and nine were women, which reflects the gender prevalence of the disease. According to data from the Infectious Disease Unit, for every three infected males, one female is infected. Of the group of men surveyed, 76 declared themselves homosexual, 33 heterosexual, and 14 bisexual. Regarding their marital status, 78 were single, 16 were married, 21 lived in free union, two were widowed, one was separated, and five did not answer this question.

In-depth Interviews

Fifteen patients participated in an in-depth interview, in which they were asked about nine topics: their profile; their belief or not in God; the qualities they assigned to God; their daily relational experience with God; the possible relationship that God has with their illness; their membership in a church; their participation in church; what they would expect from their church in relation to their situation; and the role of their ministers or priests.

Data from In-depth Interviews

The profiles of these 15 people interviewed were as follows:

- Ten were men and five were women;
- Three of them were homosexual, three bisexual, and nine heterosexual;
- Their ages ranged between 24 and 70 years;
- They were diagnosed between 1995 and 2013;
- Eleven were single and four were married;
- Many had children, while others did not or had no interest in having children because although they would like to have them, they fear that they will be born infected with HIV.
- Fourteen were Colombians and one was foreign.

These data, apparently simple, are very important because they are revealing, in relation to the social imaginaries that we usually have: HIV occurs in both sexes. It is true that most people living with HIV/AIDS are usually men, but there are also a considerable number of women (one third) who were infected by men and have in turn infected other men. Therefore, it is not only a disease for men. In addition, in the first years of the onset of the disease, HIV was associated with homosexual behavior. In addition, although the homosexual population seems to remain the majority affected by this virus—as we generally confirmed in this research—there are also participants that declared themselves as bisexuals. For some, this expression is used as a way to avoid confessing their homosexuality.

The wide spectrum of ages is striking; while young people are more likely not to protect themselves in their sexual activity, it is surprising that there are also older people who are infected. This demonstrated that HIV does not respect age or sex. It can affect anyone.

Regarding the time of diagnosis, cases diagnosed 20 or more years ago were observed. This confirms that with timely detection and care, the HIV-positive patient can have a high quality of life for many years. It is not, therefore, an unbearable and terminal disease. The fact that most of the patients are single does not mean that they do not have children. Several participants said that they had children out of wedlock. What is striking is that several respondents would also have liked to have children, but once they discovered they were HIV positive, they feared that their children would be born HIV positive and so chose not to have children. This coincided with the homosexual population, who do not want or have not thought about having children.

Without exception, everyone affirmed to believe in God. This response might not be surprising, given that the research was in a traditional and socially religious context. However, this does draw attention to what usually happens in the first phase of a newly discovered disease, when patients question God ("why me?"), feel that they have been given a divine punishment question, or break with their beliefs. Among the qualities that they attribute to God, we uncovered the following: care and protection (5), father figure (4), being of light (2), teacher (2), the greatest (2), supreme and powerful (2), and good, wonderful, energy, it is real, it is not a myth, it is not ideology, it is love, a friend, it does not punish, it is everything for me, and it is tranquility (all 1).

Of all the interviewees, only one (at some point in the interview) said: "God forgot me." Most people expressed their relationship with God not as a relationship of cold, hard facts, but as a positive and pleasant experience. It is also important to draw attention to the recurrence of the two most common characteristics. Five participants indicated that God cares for and protects them. Four considered him a father, a figure associated with protection and care.

They expressed their everyday relationship with God in the following ways: I feel His presence (10); I talk with Him or pray (6); He gives me strength (3); it is a close relationship (2); He has spoken to me in my dreams or through others (2); when someone is well I forget Him, when someone is ill I remember Him (2); and I discuss things with Him, I love God, I am more spiritual, and I ask permission (all 1).

Above, we mentioned the impact of perceiving the warmth of the participants' relationship with God. This was strongly corroborated. He is a close God, whose strength and presence are felt, who is loved and with whom one has a daily colloquial relationship: one dreams of Him, talks to Him, argues with Him, asks His permission. Some of these contrast with forgetting God when someone is well and remembering Him when someone is unwell.

Regarding the relationship with their illness that they might attribute to God, the participants stated: what happened is not His fault, it is my own (9), He made this happen for my good (7), it brought me closer to Him (7), He does not leave me dying (3), I thank Him for what happened to me (3), it helped me to change, to realize what really matters (2), and I denied His existence and, I reconsidered my beliefs (all 1). It is surprising that most of the participants exonerated God from all responsibility for their illness. This awareness of being responsible for acquiring HIV and assuming it as something good, for which they even gave thanks, helped them to change and to come closer to God; this is very striking, as it reflects maturity in the face of reality, at both the psychological and spiritual levels.

Of the interviewees, 13 were members of Catholics churches, one was from a Christian evangelical church, and one did not participate in any church. They confirmed or corroborated that Colombia is mostly Christian and Catholic.

Their relationship with the church (temple or institution) manifested in the following ways: I go from time to time (5), I do not attend any service (5), fear of being rejected by the church (3), very far away, discriminates (2), rigid and closed, I try not to go, I am not a practitioner, a friend motivates me to attend, when I go I kneel and pray, and I learned to pray mechanically (all 1). In contrast to the closeness to God in a positive relationship, this confirms another hypothesis: people often accept God, while rejecting the church. Only a third of the participants said that they went to church occasionally. This cannot be ignored. In addition, only one third stated that the church is tangentially important to them. In addition, it is striking that they are aware that they see the church as something distant, rigid, discriminating, that instills fear, and is self-enclosed.

Their most distant relationship with the church corresponds to what they expect from it: accompaniment, listening, understanding (6), support, encouragement (6), spiritual help (2), seeking to sensitize (2), not to judge (2), moral and psychological help, support the poorest, does not press or force change, gets out there, and helps those who need it (all 1). If they were curious about an effective divorce from church, the church is granted an important role and is asked to perform the tasks of listening and providing support, moral help, understanding, and encouragement. It may be that for some issues, the church does not enjoy credibility, but it does offer these services.

Regarding priests, the responses from the participants included, I did not want to talk to anyone (2), and I would like to talk to them (1). Priests were practically absent from the discussions. Only three people alluded to priests. Two avoided meeting and talking to them. Only one talked with them. The survey did not reveal this explicitly, but this would be a good reason for the church to question itself in relation to this population group.

Workshops

Another instrument used in the research was the workshops, which aimed to generate interactive spaces with patients and build knowledge through the active and creative contribution of each person participating in the research. The workshops were held with two aims in mind: training and research. There were 15 workshops, in which an average of 30 people participated per workshop. In seven workshops, each of the research categories was included. In the other eight, they worked on an activity that we call "art therapy."[14]

In the three workshops that were held to address spirituality, nearly thirty patients participated. In the first workshop, we talked about the problem to be researched, which initially considered how to investigate the way God is revealed in PLWHA, an issue that was very abstract. It was proposed to change this to "What characterizes the experience of PLWHA." After a lengthy discussion, the patients did not feel comfortable because they considered talking about their religious experience, in some way, to link them to a church and religion. Several members of the group were opposed to this because at some point in their lives, they felt stigmatized. Finally, they proposed spirituality, a category that managed to capture everyone's feelings, insofar as they felt less religious and more universal. Almost at the end, a man who was approximately 40 years old contributed the following:

> I consider myself a spiritual person, but not religious. I do not usu-
> ally go to mass or confess, but I have joined Jesus. I read His word.
> I listen to programs on the radio and I pray a lot. It is just that for a
> person living with HIV/AIDS it is very fucked up [difficult]to live
> without support ("a palo seco").[15]

14. This workshop was conducted by Ángela Rivas and took place on Saturday mornings during the three years of the research.

15. Witness by Martha, workshop n° 1, April 2015 (the name was changed to preserve

Therefore, in the second workshop, which was called "a palo seco," the objective was to try to understand through the daily experiences of patients what it means to "viver a palo seco;" that is, without the support of a spiritual experience. The contributions were collected in an observational format, which some of the group volunteers had previously prepared and helped us to collect. The most significant part of this second workshop can be summarized in the following sentence of a patient:

> We all have spirituality. Living without spirituality is like living without drinking water: one dries out, becomes dehydrated, and even dies.[16]

In the third workshop, we worked on the characteristics of spirituality. The workshop was very interesting because it demonstrated the deep relationship between their religious experience (mostly Catholic) and their spirituality. A few belonged to Christian evangelical churches, and only two or three claimed not to belong to any church. Among the most significant and reiterative contributions, especially of men who have sexual relations with other men, the experience of stigmatization stood out. From a young age, they felt singled out by their own families because of their sexual identity. Some of them claimed to feel as if they were God's mistake.

In the art therapy workshops, the connection between the recycling process and life in times of crisis was discussed. The workshop was organized around three categories: (1) Reduce, (2) Reuse, and (3) Recycle. Reduction was connected with learning to reduce fears and faults to help the participants free themselves from their life situation. They could reduce negative emotions and look for practical solutions to assist with integral healing. Reuse made it possible to bring to the present the values that they had grown up with, in order to become stronger and to project a better future. Reusing the materials for artistic creations allowed them to recreate their emotions and feelings. Recycling helped to collect all the good that exists in each participant, to "re-imagine" and create new possibilities. The results of these workshops were concretized in sculptures that were presented at international events in which they participated during the research period. These objects of art reflected the ability of art to express pain and to project alternatives for change.

---

anonymity).

16. Witness by Rafael, workshop n° 2, May 2015 (the name was changed to preserve anonymity).

Two workshops were held on the "body," and approximately 15 people participated. The participants reflected on their bodies and corporeity through two exercises. The first was "*Mi mapa corporal*," [My bodily map] a painting technique, and the second was, "*Una carta a mi cuerpo*," [A letter to my body] a writing technique. These exercises enabled the participants to acquire a better theoretical understanding of the body and corporal categories. From the experiential methodology, the patients recognized their body as a relational unit, with themselves, with others, and with the transcendent. They also highlighted the importance of caring, dignifying, and respecting their body. Some of the questions asked included: What parts of my body do I like? Which ones do I not like? To what extent does the knowledge, recognition, and acceptance of my body influence the way I communicate with my environment? Has disease influenced the way I perceive my body? Would I like to change something about my body? How do others perceive my body?

Two workshops were held on sexuality, to help recognize the fears and difficulties faced by PLWHA in relation to their sexuality, before and after diagnosis. In these workshops, two exercises were conducted. The first was semantic, related to the modes of expression of PLWHA. The second was related to the difficulties faced by patients with regard to their spirituality and sexuality. In both cases, the information was collected using recordings made by the patients and recordings of observer-members of the research team. The two sources of information were recorded in electronic files and as photographs.

Life Stories, Field Diaries, and Focus Groups

We also used the life story,[17] field diary,[18] and focus group methodologies to obtain qualitative information in relation to the experience of HIV of the research participants. Life stories constitute narrative genres that also include biographical stories. This genre is used by social sciences research with the "purpose of reconstructing personal experiences that connect with each other" and "individuals interacting in families, groups, and institutions."[19]

The personal narrative is a biographical research tool that "consists of the unfolding of a person's experiences over time, which includes a conscious and unconscious selection of memories of events or situations

17. Sautu, "Estilos y prácticas," 21–60.

18. Acero, "El diario de campo."

19. Sautu, "Estilos y prácticas," 21.

in which she participated directly or indirectly."[20] The tool allows us to recover experiences of people who have lived a common reality in different ways: "Today, taking on the challenge of working with life stories presupposes this inheritance: language no longer works as inert material, in which the researcher can search for those content related to a hypothesis or his/her own interest . . . but, on the contrary, as a word event that conveys a dialogical and existential complexity."[21]

According to Acero, "The field journal is the instrument that allows us to interrogate and unravel the meaning of reality, constituting the biographical witness of our experience."[22] The field diary records the circumstances of the investigation process as follows: "The field journal will become the means to analyze, categorize, and therefore critically review our [natural modes] of performance."[23]

About 12 patients, students of the School of Theology, and professionals attached to the research participated in the focus group. During the eight sessions, they talked about their perceptions in relation to listening and spiritual guidance, and their connections with the life experiences of PLWHA. The focus group began with two stories from the Gospel of Luke: the parable of the Good Samaritan (Luke 10:25–37) and the meeting of Jesus with the disciples of Emmaus (Luke 24:13–35). From these, several questions were posed. The opinions of the participants were collected, and the relationships they had during significant moments in their lives were discussed. Two life histories were reconstructed. The data narrated by the different patients, at different moments of the process, was qualitatively examined. It should be noted that throughout the three years that the research lasted, there were different venues for the research activities that contributed to the knowledge, depth, and qualification of the methodology and research subjects.[24]

20. Sautu, "Estilos y prácticas," 22.

21. Arfuch, O espaço biográfico, 258.

22. Acero, "El diario de campo," 17.

23. Acero, "El diario de campo," 17.

24. Congreso Latinoamericano de Pastoral de la Salud y Humanización, convocado por el CELAM y el Centro Camiliano de Pastoral de la Salud, Bogotá, October 31 and November 1, 2014 workshop, "Tools of the IAP applied to our research"; facilitator, Dr. María Cristina Quevedo; Bogotá, PUJ, February 2015. SAVE tools workshop course, "Guide for the prevention of HIV/AIDS"; facilitator, HnaDee Smith; Chinauta, February 25–27, 2015. IV Ibero-American Congress on Gender and Religion, convened by the Escuela Superior de Teología–EST, São Leopoldo, Brazil, August 8–10, 2015.

Theoretical Framework

The categories that framed this research were spirituality, corporeality, sexuality, and gender. We gave a presentation on each of these topics, without covering them in their entirety, but as fundamental statements to guide our reflection.

It is increasingly important to affirm that the human being is a complex subject, joined together in a unit. Subsequently, "comprehensive education" was described as "the continuous, permanent, and participatory process that seeks to harmoniously and coherently develop each and every one of the dimensions of the human being: ethical, spiritual, cognitive, affective, communicative, aesthetic, corporal and socio-political, in order to achieve its full realization in society. We see the human being as one, and at the same time, multidimensional, quite diverse as a body, and at the same time fully integrated and articulated in a unity."[25] This is fundamental for the work that concerns us.

The body alludes to the corporal dimension, spirituality to the spiritual dimension, and sexuality to one aspect of the affective dimension. When we separate them into dimensions, "we are doing a mental abstraction to separate what is inseparable from the human being, but we do it to understand it better and study it in the same way."[26] It is, therefore, a purely arbitrary fragmentation or division for pedagogical and didactic purposes, given that the treatment is daily and ordinarily employed; but, we are fully aware that they are inseparable. To reiterate, we are units of body, spirit, and sexuality.

Thus, when we speak of the spiritual dimension, we allude to the "possibility that human beings have of transcending their existence to open themselves up to universal values, beliefs, doctrines, rites, and convictions that give a global and profound meaning to the experience of one's life, and from it to the world, history, and culture."[27] This means that due to that unrestricted desire to know and inquire, the human being, when formulating

---

Commemoration of the international day for the fight against HIV/AIDS, Bogotá, December 1, 2015. II Congress of Latin American and German theologians, "Spaces of peace, signs of the times," convened by Teologanda, Buenos Aires, March 28–31, 2016. The course, "Management of mourning and accompaniment," PUJ Continuing Education, April 18–23, 2016. The course, "Accompaniment and Spiritual Discernment," PUJ Continuing Education, May 16–21, 2016.

25. Acodesi, *La formación integral*.

26. Acodesi, *La formación integral*, 15.

27. Acodesi, *La formación integral*, 17.

fundamental questions like "Who am I? Why do I exist?" (and, therefore, seeking to find meaning in life), is doomed to transcendence, to the totally Other.

It should be remembered here that the adjective "spiritual" comes from the Latin *spiritus*, which means breath, with its equivalents *pneuma* in Greek and *ruach* in Hebrew; terms associated with the intelligible "logos," that is, the question of the raison d'être of human existence. Therefore, when using the word spiritual, one is alluding to self-awareness, reflection, or unity and the perfect identity that is the constitutive personality.

When we speak of the corporal dimension, we are referring to the "possibility that the human being has to manifest themselves in their body and with their body, to recognize the other and to be a 'material' presence from their body. It also includes the possibility of generating and participating in training processes and physical and motor development."[28]

In the Platonic, and particularly the Neoplatonic tradition, spirit and body are separated and opposed to one other, leading to a dualistic conception with radical Manichean connotations that the former is good and the latter bad. The former is a hostage imprisoned within the latter, waiting for death for its full liberation and authentic happiness. The former was pure, the latter material and corruptible; transcendent and immanent; *logos* and *bios*; divine and human; good and evil. In those days, we had a body but never, as we do now, with the full conviction that we are a body, in indivisible unity with the spirit. However, we will have to refine our thinking conceptually, distinguishing corporality, corporeity, and body. Corporality refers to the relationships that the human being establishes with their natural, social, and cultural environment. Corporeity is the presence and manifestation of the human, to which the human being assumes their body and allows it to express itself. In addition, *body* alludes to that organic biological matter, ordinarily opposed to the spirit as we noted above, but which in reality essentially, and vitally, constitutes the human being, without which one cannot think, understand, or explain.

Finally (at least for the three dimensions that we are dealing with), when we speak of the affective dimension we mean the "set of potentialities and manifestations of the psychic life of the human being that encompasses the experience of emotions, feelings, and sexuality, as well as the way they relate to themselves and others. It includes the whole reality of the person, helping them to build themselves as a social being and to be

28. Acodesi, *La formación integral*, 18.

a co-participant in the context in which they live."[29] In this sense, it is not a broken bag where everything fits, including personality traits, cultural practices, values, feelings, emotions, and sexuality.

Evidently, sexuality is one component of the affective dimension of the human being. Undoubtedly, it is a constituent part of it, a construction, and not only a biological pre-determination in which several components interact to assist with understanding and analyzing humanity: biological, psychological, relational, sociocultural, and existential. In this way, spirit-body-sexuality is an inseparable triad within the human being. We are, therefore, all a sexualized spiritual body.

Spirituality

The category "spirituality" appears in important reflections of philosophical anthropology, specifically in definitions of the human. The history of knowledge in the West refers to Plato's ancient definitions of the human, where the psyche and the soma and the union of the soul and the body, constitute the human and define the human. Is the body the temple that welcomes the psyche? Alternatively, is the body the grave that buries the psyche? Would the body then be the prison of the soul? Is the body immanence and is the psyche transcendence within the human? What characteristics and components does this psyche have that constitute and define the human? These are some of the questions that Plato addresses in dialogues about the psyche, such as those in *Cratylus*, *The Republic*, and *Phaedrus*, and which some consider to be among the first anthropologies and psychologies that included the first definitions of the human. In Plato, the psyche, or soul, is related to the spirit and to that which is also *anima*, and which animates us, which allows us to live, move, and reason, and which links us with entities and areas of the divine, sacred, and transcendent. Viewed from contemporary anthropological perspectives, spirituality is related to the construction of social bonds and meaning, with the production of meaning and with the links that we establish with others and with ourselves.

Spirituality, viewed from such anthropological perspectives, rather than being linked to the transcendent, would allow us to bond socially, to make sense of our relationships, and to endow us with meanings about who we are. Thus, spirituality is both collective and subjective, as we possess a spirituality that defines each one of us. It defines our interiority and gives

---

29. Acodesi, *La formación integral*, 17.

meaning to our subjectivity. At the same time, we have a collective spirituality that unites, enables our belonging, and gives meaning to our links. So, we say that we share a family spirit, a group spirit, a cultural spirit, a spirit of nation, and a spirit that ties us to a territory. Spirituality is something social and individual that gives meaning to our individual body and our social body, something that allows us to relate to ourselves and to others.

Talking about spirituality in the context of HIV is a complex issue because spirituality is an unprecedented and original adventure for every human being. Spirituality is the breath of life that promotes meaning, faith, and the dynamism of hope. It integrates us, as corporeal and sexed beings, in relation to ourselves, with others, with nature, and with God; and this opens our eyes to the suffering of others. It creates solidarity, makes us aware that we are not alone, and to the extent that we leave ourselves and go to meet the Other, allows us to begin to heal our wounds.[30]

From the viewpoint of PLWHA, spirituality translates into that experience of unshakable faith that people demonstrate in extreme situations, and that manifests itself as a sense of life. As articulated in the discipleship of Jesus of Nazareth, spirituality strengthens values and attitudes that help maintain health, resist adversity, and motivate us to restart vital projects.

Previously, without losing the universal perspective that spirituality has, we placed ourselves in the Christian spiritual experience; therefore, the spirit has been a gift and a grace through Jesus and the Father, and it is the spirit of Jesus. When we open ourselves to His presence, He also opens us to His immeasurable mystery of compassion, kindness, and solidarity. The spirit of the risen Jesus signifies, encourages, and strengthens all the pursuits we undertake. Therefore, if we want to experience a living spirituality that contributes to the reconstruction of vital projects, we will have to inquire about what most helps PLWHA in their processes of recovering integral health. This requires them to have faith in themselves and in others, to face life with courage and without fear, and to feel loved by God, and thus, to love without measure.

Body and Corporeity

Various philosophical, sociological, anthropological, and feminist perspectives have dealt with bodies as complex material and symbolic entities, composed of flesh and speech, and tangible and intangible elements. We speak then of bodies shaped by nature and by the culture of the human

30. Casaldáliga and Vigil, *Espiritualidad de la Liberación*, 27.

being, bodies with which we are born, that are given and innate, but in which we also intervene, build, mean, and name, always in a collective and subjective way. These bodies are places, in many ways, and according to Michel Foucault, they are places where subjectivity is established. In anthropology and sociology, they are places of cultural, symbolic, and social intervention, and they are political places in feminist theory as places of theoretical, political, subjective, and identity construction.

Some philosophers, such as Gilles Deleuze, trace the philosophy of the body to Spinoza and his questions about the powers of the body, what a body can do, and the political power of the body. This was in a seventeenth-century philosophical, theological, and scientific milieu that despised the body, its powers, and its possibilities. In their reflections on philosophy and the social sciences, other philosophers, such as Michel Foucault and Sandra Pedraza, consider Nietzsche an important source for the genealogy of the body. For Nietzsche, the body, and how power manifests itself in the body, was important, as this is the power that dominates and makes the body possible. Furthermore, Marcel Mauss wrote an essay in the 1930s entitled "The Techniques of the Body." This work is important in the anthropology and sociology of the body, because Mauss poses how our bodies, our ways of walking, swimming, and resting, how the ways we present the body we develop, respond to cultural processes of learning and the socialization of bodies. Mauss proposes the concept of corporal hexis, a concept that allows us to think about how our bodily ways, our bodily movements, respond to socially acquired dispositions that emerge every day and are incorporated and naturalized.

Later, sociologists such as Pierre Bourdieu thought that the objective schemes of perception and collective organization, those of individual bodies, and principles of subjective vision and action are integrated. Bourdieu talks about how bodies are socially constructed and of the processes of incorporation. The anthropology of the body is interested in the effect of culture on the body, in the effect of worldviews, of meanings, of languages, and of institutions on people's bodies. In these approaches, the body is seen as a subjective and collective space, as a space of domination and potency, as a space for health and disease, as a space for harmony and war, as a space for pleasure and pain, and as a masculine and feminine space.

Feminist theory has been interested in sexed bodies, in the bodies of men and women, in bodies turned into objects and in the violated bodies of women, in bodies that are seen as legitimate, legible, and that matter, and in those bodies that are treated as illegitimate, that are illegible, and that often do not matter. Accordingly, feminism has built theories on the exploitation and forms of rebellion of sexed bodies, medicalized, racialized, classified, and oppressed in different ways, and in different rebellious and liberated forms. Feminist theory is, then, a political theory of bodies.

Sexuality

For Michel Foucault and feminists such as Monique Wittig, Gayle Rubin, Teresa de Lauretis, Judith Butler, and Beatriz Preciado, sexuality could be defined as a device of power, a complex device of collective and subjective power made up of bodies, histories, institutions, discourses, languages, categories, differences, laws, desires, controls, leaks, representations, and struggles. Sexuality would be defined as a political regime that produces categories, regulations, hierarchies, names, and discourses. In addition, sexuality produces subjects: we subject ourselves to sexuality, and at the same time, sexuality subjects us, coerces us, and classifies us.

Fundamental principles of masculine domination and female subordination are established in sexuality: sexuality as reproduction, as a manifestation of masculine violence, as a commodity, and female sexuality as a pathology have been important areas of feminist reflection. The establishment of heterosexuality as a norm and as a model of thought has also been approached by feminism. This system, this regime, and this heterosexual thinking produce a series of bodies, categories, subjects, and experiences that are abject, affected and stigmatized, and that are others, which establish themselves as difference and contrast with what is considered normal, natural, healthy, good, useful, orderly, correct, and straight. Some heterosexual bodies matter, and other non-heterosexual bodies do not matter. In this research, we analyzed the impact of HIV on sexualities socially considered as masculine, feminine, normal, clean, abnormal, non-normative, homosexual, and contaminated.

Gender

Gender refers to power relations between masculine and feminine, to forms of classification and differentiation, and to social, linguistic, and cultural constructions based on sexual differences. Gender has been introduced into the social sciences and anthropology through political and theoretical feminist practices that sought to question the superiority of men in public, political, academic, and economic spaces, as well as to denounce and transform the conditions of sexual violence and inequality experienced by many women in the world. The gender category allows us to reflect on the differences between men and women, on the inequalities between the masculine and the feminine, on the privileges of the masculine in the production of knowledge, and on the undervaluation of women in the social sciences. Gender is a political category, to the degree that it refers to power, inequality, and the hierarchies established around, in our case, masculinity and femininity, the masculine and feminine bodies, male and female sexualities, and the spirituality of men and women.

In this research, the category of gender allows us to reflect on the different ways of assuming life with a positive diagnosis of HIV/AIDS in men and women, and on power relations and the hierarchies implicit in these differences. The category of gender allows us to analyze the differences that exist within the masculine and feminine. Particularly, in this case, it allows us to analyze the differences between queer men, homosexual men, heterosexual men, young men, and older men, in their experiences with HIV/AIDS.

Results

A Characterization of the "Subject" Population of the Research

Data that allow us to characterize the subject or interlocutor population in this investigation have already been made available. We also intend to continue deepening our understanding of other sources of enrichment for the populations in the project's sharing network.

Views from a Gender Perspective: Men, Women, and HIV

On the social and demographic characterizations, most of the people who made up our sample (93 percent) were adult men. Our survey demonstrates that there is still a high prevalence of men living with HIV. Although more women are acquiring the virus, HIV in our national and regional context still has a male face or, better yet, male faces; herein, we refer to various forms of masculinities and of being a man. In the epidemiological figures, health services, memories of the disease, and social imagination, a very strong association of HIV with the masculine body prevails, and in particular, the bodies of men, of homosexual men, adult men, white men, and mestizos. Recently, heterosexual men are also recognized and quantified as vulnerable bodies with HIV.[31]

The implications of HIV in women are very different with respect to the use of health services, stigma and discrimination, establishment and reestablishment of support networks, family experiences, and experiences with the sacred. This is because a diagnosis of HIV/AIDS in a female body is related to an androcentric structure of female body dominance, which regulates sexuality and marks female bodies. The representations and metaphors of HIV associate it with promiscuity, multiple relationships and sexual partners, and sexual activity, which is socially sanctioned and recognized differently in men and women. Due to the social sanctions that follow from the stigmatization of female sexuality in our androcentric structure of sexuality, it is more difficult for a woman with a HIV diagnosis to establish support networks, demand rights and health services, and live subjectively and collectively with HIV/AIDS. This may be related to the low percentage of women in our sample (7 percent) that was collected in the institutional context of access to healthcare.

In our society, hetero-normative male sexuality has always been more recognized, allowed, and accepted. There are specific public places for its manifestation that include porn movie theaters, street prostitution, pornographic materials, and the mass media. The female bodies and images that appear in these spaces are objects of desire, for pleasure, and for the masculine sexuality, which is configured as the main producer and consumer of sexuality. Permissible female sexuality has been confined to the domestic sphere, to reproduction, to being the object of male sexuality, and to being an object of knowledge and clinical scientific control. Due to the sexualization of the virus, a woman saying she has HIV is like manifesting her own promiscuity, and this is more reproached in women than in men in our cultural contexts. HIV is not just a virus, a state of the immune system, or a biological entity. It is also a sign, a symbol that communicates sexuality, contamination, and abjection; it is a meaning, socially constructed, as are all meanings. In the survey, 15 percent of the participants claimed feeling stigmatized for living with HIV in their bodies. This figure shows how history is being updated, how the practices of signification and stigmatization of the 1980s are somehow being maintained.

The experience or prospect of being a mother also complicates an HIV positive diagnosis for women and living with HIV as a woman. The

31. UNFPA, *Factores de vulnerabilidad.*

fear for the health of the child, of being rejected by them, or of not being able to be a mother are issues that cross the subjectivities and spiritualties of women. These issues appeared in the data and reflections that we collected in our project. In addition, the female participants had stable partners at the time of diagnosis, which often led to romantic disappointment due to suspicions of infidelity and much confusion. Since they were heterosexual and monogamous, they believed that they were almost immune to HIV/AIDS, a belief that violently collapsed at the time of diagnosis.

Many of the men participating in the survey (63 percent) labelled themselves as homosexual. As we mentioned at the beginning of the text, because of HIV's history, epidemiology, representations, metaphors, and linked prejudices, it has been seen as a homosexual disease, related to homosexual bodies and political groups, since the middle of the 1980s and up to the present. In a workshop on gender and sexuality conducted within the framework of our project, one participant stated that for a homosexual man, receiving a positive HIV diagnosis was not unusual. This statement demonstrates how these identities, associations, and sexual practices relate (collectively and subjectively) to HIV, producing particular forms of stigma and discrimination associated with the disease, but paradoxically also creating coping mechanisms and strategies to deal with the implications of a positive HIV diagnosis.

A smaller percentage of men participating in the sample (30 percent) defined themselves as heterosexual. This has many implications for the lives of these men, in matters such as receiving a collective and subjective diagnosis, linking to support networks, and experiencing stigma and discrimination. The shame, fear, and stigmatization experienced by heterosexual men diagnosed with HIV/AIDS were expressed in our workshops, interviews, and dialogue. In our project, it was very important to approach these different masculine identities, ways of being a man, and relationships of men with HIV/AIDS sensitively, as our goal was to develop a perspective of gender, informed by an analysis of the different ways of being a man with HIV/AIDS.

Social Class, Health, Support Networks, and HIV/AIDS: Nexuses Reinforced and Nexuses Broken Down

Most of the people surveyed belonged to survey strata two and three, with respective percentages of 28 percent and 48 percent; 15 percent were situated in stratum four. Much of the sample (91 percent) was made up of the middle strata of the population. Inevitably, the issue of location in social space and class influences the experiences of PLWHA in many ways. The Colombian health system offers different services according to social class. This has implications for access to services, quality of care, and respect. Of the sample, 90 percent received contributory health care, and 10 percent received subsidized health care. Of the respondents, 36 percent claimed to receive proper care, and 62 percentsaid that they received excellent care at San Ignacio University Hospital. Overall, the availability of access was related to their social class.

Regarding suggestions for improving HIV health care, 19 percent of the respondents suggested strengthening psychological, spiritual, and group support; 12 percent suggested improving administrative matters; and 12 percent suggested improving the time of care. They also demanded more information.

Of the respondents, 37 percent had an income that was two or three times higher than the minimum wage; 31 percent received the minimum wage; and 22 percent had an income of more than four times the minimum wage. In addition, 38 percent of the respondents had an undergraduate and postgraduate education, and 26 percent had completed technical studies.

Of the people surveyed, 70 percent claimed to have been employed at the time of diagnosis, and 66 percent said they were currently employed. Such a statistic could raise the question of whether, even today, a diagnosis of HIV implies exclusion from employment and loss of work due to stigma and discrimination. We are currently working on this question, mainly among professionals, people who have paid jobs, do skilled labor, and who are middle class.

Regarding the support network, 33 percent affirmed that their support network is made up of their family, 15 percent claimed it was their partner or ex-partner, and 13 percent affirmed that they do not have a support network. These figures tell us about processes of solidarity and loneliness around HIV, which is important to approach from sociological, anthropological, and public health perspectives. It is also significant that 13 percent affirmed that nobody forms their support network; it is possible that a positive diagnosis of HIV generates social ruptures, breakdown of support networks, and loneliness. Patching these broken social ties would be an important task for sociological, anthropological, and spiritual approaches to the experiences of PLWHA.

Skin Color: Ethnicity and HIV

Of all the respondents, 32 percent recognized themselves as white, 65 percent as mestizo, and 1 percent as black. HIV also has connotations linked to race and ethnicity. In the Colombian context, it is directly linked to segments of the white and mestizo population. The implications of HIV in racialized bodies such as Afro or indigenous bodies would be interesting to analyze because, in addition to the sexual connotations, the HIV experience would be related to structures of race, ethnicity, cultural difference, and racism in the Colombian context.

Love, Sexuality, and HIV: Forms of Company and Loneliness

Of the sample, 54 percent stated that they had a partner and 46 percent were single. Some participants in the survey stated that HIV is a limitation to having a partner and developing a sexual and emotional life, due to the fears, complications, and stigmatization associated with HIV. Although HIV is a sexualized disease, for some, this implies the end of sexuality and affectivity and the closure of this area of experience, as if HIV contaminated and blocked this area. On the marital status of the participants, we determined the following: 62 percent were single, 20 percent lived in a nonbinding partnership, and 13 percent were married.

Several participants acknowledged experiencing sexuality and love while living with HIV. For some, HIV does not eliminate the possibility of establishing sexual and affective relationships. This area of life can be further developed with specific care and responsibilities after diagnosis. However, for most of the respondents (75 percent), the diagnosis changed their sexuality; 33 percent said that they had changed because now they are more responsible with their bodies. These processes of transition and reconfiguration of sexuality are related to spirituality, in the collective reflections of our research project. Of the respondents, 40 percent said that they currently take care of themselves through a healthy lifestyle and medical control. 18 percent affirmed that they take care of themselves by using condoms and attending medical control sessions.

Regarding the question of how their body feels, 36 percent of the participants said the same as before, 13 percent answered that they were indifferent, and 15 percent said they felt stigmatized in relation to the diagnosis of HIV. Thus, a representative percentage of the sample were stigmatized by HIV/AIDS. Despite the progress that has been made in reducing stigma and discrimination, these factors continue to appear in the lives of people living with the virus.

Spirituality and HIV/AIDS: Invisible and Indispensable Forces

Of the sample, 92 percent claimed to be believers; 66 percent were Catholic and 10 percent evangelical Christian. Of the respondents, 45 percent believed in a merciful and compassionate God, and 16 percent in a God who is both a father and a mother. Many people talked about the importance of the sacred in their process after diagnosis and continuing with their lives. Regarding the spiritual characterization: 29 percent have faith in living, 24 percent take more responsibility for themselves and with others, and 23 percent have spirituality and meaning in their lives. Thus, to many people, the sacred gives them strength and encourages them to continue on pathways of life, as if HIV had taken away power and light, while the spiritual generated power and light.

It is interesting to see how, for many of the people surveyed, the diagnosis of HIV and the subjective and collective acknowledgment of the diagnosis implies a change, rupture, or transformative process that manifests itself in different areas of their experience. It affects issues such as the spiritual, affective, sexual, and relationships with society and with one's own body. HIV, and the multiple and complex life transitions that it implies, is an important topic in research and action regarding the relationship between HIV and the spiritual.

The relationship between the spiritual and HIV has been little explored in studies conducted on the disease, as these studies emphasize clinical issues, rights, sexuality and gender, as well as political and economic aspects of the disease, ignoring the areas of the spiritual that affect the experiences and lives of PLWHA.

Silence: A Way to Confront HIV/AIDS

In addition to the stigmas and social representations that we noted in the previous section, in the history of HIV/AIDS, we also find a series of political, material, and spiritual effects in collectivities, corporalities, and concrete subjectivities. In the 1980s, the HIV virus and deaths from AIDS devastated the bodies and spirits of gay people, communities, and social organizations around the world. Bodies began to weaken suddenly, and opportunistic diseases appeared, such as pneumonia and, on the skin, Kaposi's sarcoma. Then came a death that was often silent, painful, lonely, and shameful. The spirits and subjectivities of the patients were destroyed along with their bodies, due to the fear, guilt, and confusion generated by this disease, which was beginning to be associated with non-normative forms of sexuality. In addition, the spirits of the people close to them, of friends, of companions, and of the partners of the sick and dead were also strongly affected by the pain of loss, by not having answers from governments or health institutions, for feeling that an unknown disease was killing them and that perhaps they would be soon be affected next. These spiritual, collective, and subjective effects of HIV/AIDS, in the past and in the present, are issues that especially interest us in this research project.

The responses to these deaths were diverse. At times, the responses were guilt, fear, solitude, and silence on the part of people affected by the disease and the people closest to them. At other times, public mobilizations were organized by groups of homosexual men in large cities of the United States and Europe. Collectives, such as Act Up New York, Act Up Paris, and Queer Nation, demonstrated against the silence surrounding AIDS at that time, as it was determined that the silence of victims and their families, in the United States, and of health institutions had contributed to the death rate. "Silence = death" was, in effect, one slogan that began to appear on posters, banners, and in public demonstrations. Breaking the silence and making AIDS public and political was one of the first goals of these mobilizations.[32]

In our interviews with PLWHA, they expressed the need to talk about their situation, to be heard, and to be accompanied spiritually. Currently, thirty years after the disease emerged in the 1980s, the testimonies of PLWHA reveal that it remains important to break the silence and overcome stigmas. Spaces of listening and spiritual accompaniment were important venues during this research project. Such active and participatory spaces have promoted dialogue and spirituality and generated knowledge, proposals, and transformations.

Art, images, performance, and theater in public spaces were important strategies of homosexual groups in the 1980s, who painted red hands on the walls of state buildings and health institutions, using slogans such as "The State has blood on its hands." In public places and where large turnouts were expected, in plazas and mass transit stations, they placed coffins with naked bodies inside as a way to denounce deaths due to AIDS

32. Llamas, *Construyendo identidades*.

and as a strategy of information and creation of social awareness about the phenomenon.[33] Another significant citizen mobilization in some cities of the United States was to weave large quilts with patches with the names of people who had died from HIV/AIDS. Artistic manifestations were very important in these historical processes of politicization and denunciation of HIV/AIDS in the 1980s and 1990s. In our research project, we also included this artistic perspective, by creating sculptures, masks, mandalas, and plays[34] that represent the experiences of living and coexisting with HIV, as related to corporalities, sexualities, and spiritualties.

In the 1990s, in Colombia and Latin America in general, homosexual groups began to demand rights to health care for PLWHA. Then, at the beginning of the twenty-first century, trans women organized themselves. They began to interact with state and health institutions, also claiming rights and expressing their specific concerns regarding HIV/AIDS and the ways in which their bodies were stigmatized by and discriminated against because of this disease, and for their non-normative gender identities. Thus, paradoxically, HIV/AIDS was an experience of pain and death that also strengthened demands for organizational, political, and sexual rights, and gender equality. However, when inquiries are made about memories of HIV/AIDS deaths in the 1980s in Colombia, many people become sentimental when recalling the deaths of their peers and close friends and remember how those deaths were a source of shame, silence, and fear. The lack of action that could have prevented these deaths was lamented and transformed into public demonstrations and political activities.

Recently, political action has encouraged people to remember deaths due to AIDS in the 1980s and 1990s because many people have not previously been able to mourn these losses. Those deaths were often shameful, and so no one was allowed to grieve for that same reason. What lives are worth crying for? Feminist philosopher Judith Butler asked this question in her book *Precarious Lives*.[35] This question arises here because many deaths from AIDS are not mourned to this day. The pain and suffering caused by this pandemic have had critical political effects on our societies. These are experiences and memories of death that have given rise to collective

33. Llamas, *Construyendo identidades*; Butler, *Precarious Lives*.

34. At the closing event for this research (the International Meeting on Theology and Sexual Health and Rights, November 29–30 and December 1, 2016 at PUJ, Bogotá) a group of patients who participated in the research presented a play titled "Cuando llega la lluvia" (When the rain comes).

35. Butler, *Precarious Lives*.

demands and that have achieved important social transformations. However, there are still deaths due to AIDS that could not be and have not been cried for. We have important questions about this. Should we forget about these deaths because of the shame and fear that they generated at the time? Alternatively, should we exercise collective memory and now cry for these deaths? What deaths are mourned and publicly remembered today? Which deaths deserve to be mourned because they do not bring us shame? Which deaths do not deserve to be mourned?

We affirmed that because pharmaceutical technologies have produced antiretroviral medicine that sustains the health and defenses of PLWHA for a long time, the experiences, and attitudes toward HIV/AIDS have changed. Some of the stigmas and metaphors associated with HIV/AIDS have changed due to the anti-stigma and anti-discrimination work of many activists, organizations, and institutions. However, despite the important clinical, symbolic, historical, and political transformations in this regard, stigmatizing and discriminatory representations of PLWHA persist. These negative social representations are manifested in strong emotional, subjective, and spiritual feelings because they generate guilt, self-rejection, and fear. They confine many people to silence and pain, just as in the 1980s.

Prospects

When the investigation was completed, there were many paths open to further exploration. The most important among them was the urgency of listening and accompanying. To that end, this research is projected towards the creation of that listening center, which effectively responds to the challenges raised here.[36]

On a medical level, notwithstanding the economic difficulties that continue to affect treatment in some countries and in large segments of the population, there are alternatives. The possibility of leading a healthy life for many years is very high. Indeed, medical science has made many advances and, today, stigma weighs more heavily than the need for scientific solutions to this disease.

At the theoretical level, the categories that are involved in this reality of HIV/AIDS convey the vision of an integral human being, a positive vision,

---

36. The Church of Sweden approved a second phase of the project to design a listening center model for a highly complex hospital, in association with the Faculty of Theology of the Pontificia Universidad Javeriana (PUJ) and the San Ignacio University Hospital.

as we have noted in the theoretical framework of this paper. Another reality is to help make this categorization permeate personal and social imaginations, in such a way that they can sustain another view of patient reality and it can create a different, healing environment for PLWHA.

As our perspective has been theological, we also want to note specific reflections on what listening and accompanying means.[37]

Listening

In the Old Testament, the word שָׁמַע (shemá) appears more than 160 times. It can mean, "hear; listen/attend/obey; abide by/accept." The importance of this word is that it does not merely mean the act of hearing; its meaning attends to the attitude of the interlocutor: "By the way, shemá can mean 'Hear.' However, the true meaning is that this word is part of the great Israelite call to worship." For example, in Deuteronomy 6:4, we find, שְׁמַע יִשְׂרָאֵל יְהוָה אֱלֹהֵינוּ יְהוָה | אֶחָד: "Hear, o Israel, the Lord our God YHWH, YHWH, the Lord is one"; and what God desires through this phrase is more than just the simple act of hearing what He would say. He wants the listener to listen carefully to what is said, understand, and do it. In Spanish, the word *to hear*, according to the *Royal Dictionary of the Spanish Language*, comes from the Latin *audīre*, and means among other things: 1) Perceive sounds with the ear; 2) Said of a person: Address the requests, pleas, or warnings from someone, or to someone; 3) Take care, or take notice, of what they are talking about; and 4) Attend to a teacher's explanation of a skill so as to learn it.

On the other hand, the word listen, according to that same dictionary, comes from the Latin *ascultāre*, and means: 1) Pay attention to what is heard; 2) Listen to, attend to a notice, advice or suggestion; 3) Use the ear to hear something; and 4) Speak or recite with affected pauses. For this reason, although the literal term for the word שָׁמַע is *to hear*, today the term hearing refers to passive auditory action: "To hear (*audīre*, in Latin) is to perceive a sound. It is something natural, physiological, not governed by our will." You hear the rain fall. Cars can be heard passing by; they are passively heard because the presence of rain or cars is perceived in the street, but they are not paid attention to. It is an involuntary act. Very often, unintentionally, we are forced to hear noises that we would prefer not to have to

---

37. A more detailed presentation on this topic is available in the master's thesis by Lima Díaz, "Renacidos por el Señor."

endure. Therefore, hearing does not have the semantic load of the Hebrew word שָׁמַע.

However, listening in this context entails an active and attentive hearing that could be closer to the *cura personalis*: The *cura personalis* is translated as 'caring for people.' Its practice is to listen attentively to a wounded interlocutor who heals his/her own spiritual wounds to the extent that he/she is heard. Listening is never a capricious or resigned act. It is the answer to a search. The doctor's instructions and advice are listened to because they are important. Likewise, the Word of God is listened to because it is transcendental. We do not listen by chance. We listen because, previously, we have wanted to listen. Listening requires attention and care. It demands that the interlocutor be fully involved so that s/he can put the received message into practice. A higher demand is required of the listener. Thus, listening is never arbitrary. It is preceded by a desire, a longing. The more intense that desire is, the more receptive is the practice of listening.

Accompany

According to the *New Latin: Spanish Etymological Dictionary and Derivative Voices*, the terms *compānĭō* and *compānĭa* come from the High Middle Ages, approximately from the fifteenth century, and were not used by classic Latin authors. *Compānĭa* means "act of eating from the same dish"; in other words, sharing the bread. *Acompañar*, according to the *Royal Dictionary of the Spanish Language*, has the following meanings, among others: 1) Be or go in the company of another or other people; 2) Put together or add something to something else; 3) Said of a thing: Exist with another or simultaneously with it; 4) Especially said of a fortune, of a state, of a quality or of a passion: To exist or to be in a person; and 5) Participate in someone's feelings. Accompanying refers to the action of not leaving another alone, of visiting, going to meet someone, of sharing a state, a path, a life, and an experience. *Compānĭa* as an act of sharing bread, has an affected transcendence, which seeks the welfare of the other in an act in which the most essential part of human subsistence is offered. Accompaniment, in its substantive form, manifests the act of accompanying, dedicating company. In addition, certainly, the first to display concern with such fortune is God Himself. God is with His people.

Humanity recognizes, throughout the salvific economy, the presence of God in action because, despite the difficulties of the human being, the Lord is the first to offer the *cura personalis*. One way to do this is through listening and accompaniment. Therefore, although no single word identifies the accompaniment of God in the Scriptures, as it does with listening, we can identify an attitude of concern by God for the human being. In God's presence we encounter humanity's desire to reach Salvation: The history of Salvation–of Revelation and Scripture–is nothing other than a dialogue. Dialogue happens between two interlocutors who speak and listen. God speaks to men, creatures, and demands of them an answer. Dialogue happens in a relationship; God establishes the initiative to relate to humanity, and God is the first to propose the *cura personalis*.

In the Word of God, one perceives how the Lord actively reveals Himself: In a metaphysical sense, revelation is nothing other than the work of God, the Creator, as such, who continuously and freely sets the position, as an action of His will and as a creative power. God participates in human life to the extent that He seeks the *cura personalis* of every human being. The Lord listens and accompanies: The Bible is truly the document of the dialogue between God and humanity. God remains attentive to listening and being heard, and the Word is the means to interact with the Lord; the Word is to be heard and practiced. In the Gospels, the central figure of listening and accompaniment is undoubtedly found in Jesus, who is presented as a merciful and charitable person when listening and accompanying. Two examples of how the word is put into practice appear in Luke, in the parable of the Good Samaritan (Luke 10:25–37), and the meeting of Jesus with the disciples of Emmaus (Luke 24:13–35).

This is where the need to heal, to take care of, to protect oneself against stigma and discrimination, and to find the saving grace of God is perceived. Listening and spiritual accompaniment are ways to access the *cura personalis*, which plays an important role for people who have been diagnosed with HIV, because it presents the grace of the merciful God. Listening and spiritual accompaniment can help one confront the realities and spiritual concerns derived from situations, such as stigma and discrimination, and their personal, social, and spiritual consequences. The configuration of sexualities includes female, male, homosexual, gay, and transgender, and so on; the affective and sexual experience: promiscuity, faithfulness in affective relationships with oneself, with other men and women; self-recognition of one's own identity and self-esteem; responsibility in sexuality: roles in affective relations, contagion, and care for oneself and others; respect for one's own body and others, caring for freedom; management of frustrations; and all other matters experienced by PLWHA.

Spirituality as an Element of Healing

The relevance of listening and accompanying, as noted above, is enriched by another of the conclusions of this research: spirituality is not a dimension outside the healing process. It provides a healing service and the strength to adhere to the treatments that this disease requires. We refer to spirituality in a broad sense, that is, not necessarily confessional, but as a dimension of meaning, of hope, and in some cases, of the true explanation of the presence of God at this difficult moment when patients face the reality of living with HIV/AIDS.

It cannot be forgotten that PLWHA are frequently invaded by a series of stressors, which begin with the confirmation of the diagnosis. They fear for their severely affected body. They fear the reaction of their family and friends. They fear the disease because their whole lives are being affected. Furthermore, many studies have demonstrated how spirituality is associated with better health and quality of life, as well as a lower propensity to commit suicide, even in patients with terminal illnesses.[38] This can have a profound effect on levels of anxiety and depression in the patient and powerfully affect their quality of life and recovery.[39]

The experience of spirituality should always be enriched by essentials that cut across its different aspects. It must be an open-eyed spirituality; that is, one that faces and acknowledges reality, and in that painful situation, is able to see the action of God, who invites one to overcome that reality, while feeling the suffering of others who also suffer.

It must also be a healing spirituality. In some confessional contexts, spirituality focuses more on the conversion of the sinful, repentance, and confession of guilt. This is not how the experience of spirituality required by PLWHA arises. It is, rather, in the dynamics of a spirituality that has mercy at its core, which does not judge but saves and which does not condemn but strengthens one to move forward.

The spirituality proposed here, assumes a positive view of the body and sexuality, in line with current theoretical developments that do not divide the human being, but rather see it in its wholeness and affirm these realities as positive dynamics for the construction of personality. It is necessary to overcome the content of spiritualties that have considered the body and sexuality as sinful, and which propose as a remedy the rejection of those dimensions of the human being. Finally, we need a lived spirituality

38. Lima Díaz, "Renacidos por el Señor," 37.
39. Lima Díaz, "Renacidos por el Señor," 40.

of listening and accompaniment by God, who is interested in the life of the person who cultivates spirituality, and of believing communities that accompany these processes. This should begin with the existence of each subject and seek the will of God for each person, more than focusing on the duties imposed by standards that do not value personal processes or consider the constraints that they entail.[40]

40. These aspects were proposed in the presentation "Spiritual experience in patients living with HIV" at the International Meeting on Theology and Sexual Health and Rights, held in Bogotá on November 29 and 30 and December 1, 2016, at the PUJ.

Bibliography

Acero, Efrén. "El diario de campo: medio de investigación del docente." *Actualidad Educativa* 13 (1996) 12–19.

ACODESI. *La formación integral y sus dimensiones*. Bogotá: Kimpres, 2002.

Anat y Shani, Abraham. *Nuevo diccionario: español–hebreo, hebreo–español*. Jerusalem: Zack, 1991.

Arfuch, Leonor. *O espaço biográfico—Dilemas da Subjetividade Contemporânea*. Rio de Janeiro: Ed. Da universidade do Estado do Rio de Janeiro, 2010. https://bibliotecaonlinedahisfj.files.wordpress.com/2015/02/arfuch-leonor-o-espac3a70-biogrc3a1fico.pdf.

Baena Bustamante. Gustavo, SJ. *Fenomenología de la Revelación: teología de la Biblia y hermenéutica*. Estella (Navarra): Verbo Divino, 2011.

Becerra, Susana. "Experiencia espiritual en pacientes que viven con VIH." Ponencia presentada en el Encuentro Internacional Teología, Salud sexual y Derechos, Bogotá, November 29–30 and December 1, 2016.

Bourdieu, Pierre. *La Dominación Masculina*. Barcelona: Anagrama, 2000. http://www.nomasviolenciacontramujeres.cl/wp-content/uploads/2015/09/Bondiu-Pierre-la-dominacion-masculina.pdf.

Butler, Judith. *Cuerpos que importan*. Buenos Aires: Paidós, 2008.

———. *El Género en Disputa*. México: Paidós—PUEG, 2001.

———. *Vida precaria. El poder del duelo y la violencia*. Buenos Aires: Paidós, 2006.

Carpenter, Eugene E., and Philip W. Comfort. *Glosario Holman de términos bíblicos*. Nashville: Broadman & Holman, 2003.

Casaldáliga, Pedro, and José MaVigil. *Espiritualidad de la Liberación*. Maliaño: Sal terrae 1992.

Cerni, Ricardo. *Antiguo Testamento Interlineal hebreo-español: Tomo I–Pentateuco*. Barcelona: Libros CLIE, 1990.

Foucault, Michel. *El poder psiquiátrico*. Buenos Aires: Fondo de Cultura Económica, 2005. https://colectivoantipsiquiatria.files.wordpress.com/2014/09/foucault-el-poder-psiquiatrico-colectivoantipsiquiatria-wordpress-com.pdf.

———. *Estética, ética y hermenéutica. ObrasEsenciales*. Barcelona: Paidós. 1999. http://exordio.qfb.umich.mx/archivos%20PDF%20de%20trabajo%20UMSNH/LIBROS%2014/Foucault%20Michel%20-%20Estetica%20Etica%20Y%20Hermeneutica%20[Sicario%20Infernal].PDF.

García Sánchez, Bárbara Yadira, and Javier Guerrero Barón. *Núcleos de Educación Social. NES*. Bogotá: Universidad Distrital Francisco José de Caldas, 2012. http://ascun.org.co/media/attachments/nucleos_de_educacion_social_nes.pdf.

Kirchner, Alicia. *La Investigación Acción Participativa*. http://forolatinoamerica.desarrollosocial.gov.ar/galardon/docs/Investigaci%C3%B3n%20Acci%C3%B3n%20Participativa.pdf.

Lantigua, Isabel. *El virus del sida comenzó a propagarse en humanos a finales del siglo XIX*. http://www.elmundo.es/elmundosalud/2008/10/01/hepatitissida/1222879761.html.

Leal, Eduardo. "La investigación acción participación, un aporte conocimiento y a la transformación de Latinoamérica, en permanente movimiento." *Revista de investigación* 67 (2009) 14–34. http://www2.scielo.org.ve/pdf/ri/v33n67/art02.pdf.

Llamas, Ricardo, ed. *Construyendo identidades. Estudios desde el corazón de la pandemia*. Madrid: Siglo XXI Editores, 1995.

Lima Díaz, David, SJ. "Renacidos por el Señor: Lineamientos teológico-pastorales para el acompañamiento espiritual a pacientes con VIH." Master's thesis, PUJ, 2017. https://repository.javeriana.edu.co/bitstream/handle/10554/36865/David%20Lima%20D%c3%adaz.pdf?sequence=4&isAllowed=y.

Lonergan, Bernard. *Método en Teología*. 6th ed. Salamanca: Sígueme, 2004.

López de Ceballos, P. *Un método para la Investigación Acción Participativa*. Madrid: Ed. Educación Popular, 1989.

Mauss, Marcel. "Las técnicas corporales." In *Sociología y Antropología*. Barcelona: Tecnos, 1971.

Ministerio de Salud y Protección Social. República de Colombia. *Panorama del VIH-SIDA en Colombia, 1983–2010. Un análisis de situación*. http://minsalud.gov.co/salud/Documents/observatorio_vih/documentos/monitoreo_evaluacion/1_vigilancia_salud_publica/b_estudios_comportamiento/PANORAMAVIHCOL_WEB.pdf.

Navia, Carmiña. "Nuevos discursos, nuevos lugares teológicos." http://www.redescristianas.net/nuevos-discursos-nuevos-lugares-teologicoscarmina-navia/.

Park, Peter. "Qué es la investigación acción participativa. Perspectivas teóricas y metodológicas." In *La investigación acción participativa. Inicios y desarrollos*, edited by María Cristiana Salazar, 135–78. Bogotá: Magisterio, 2011.

Platón. *Cratiloo del lenguaje*. Madrid: Trota, 2002.

Preciado, Beatriz. *Testo Yonqui*. Madrid: Espasa, 2008.

Rubin, Gayle. *El Género: La construcción cultural de la diferencia sexual*, edited by Marta Lamas. México: UNAM—PUEG—Miguel Ángel Porrua, 1999.

Sautu, Ruth. "Estilos y prácticas de investigación biográfica." In *El método biográfico: la reconstrucción de la sociedad a partir del testimonio de los actores*, 28–59. Buenos Aires: Belgrano, 1999.

Scott, Joan. "El Género: Una categoría útil para el análisis histórico." In *Historia y Género: Las mujeres en la Europa moderna y contemporánea*, edited by James Amelang et al, 23–58. Valencia: Alfons El Magnamin, 1990.

UNFPA—Ministerio de la Protección social. *Factores de vulnerabilidad a la infección por VIH en mujeres*. Bogotá: Universidad Nacional de Colombia, 2010.

Vélez Caro, Olga Consuelo. "El quehacer teológico y la Investigación Acción Participativa (IAP). Una reflexión metodológica." De próxima publicación en la revista *Theologica Xaveriana*, primer número del año 2017.

Wittig, Monique. *El Pensamiento Heterosexual y otros ensayos*. Madrid: Egales, 2006.

5

The Sexual Rights of Women Based on a Contextual Reading of 2 Samuel 13:1–22

A Theological Reflection on Gender-based Violence

Edgar Antonio López

THIS CHAPTER PRESENTS SOME of the results of the research, "A Theological Approach to Sexuality, Reproductive Health, and Human Rights," conducted by the Faculty of Theology at the Pontificia Universidad Javeriana and the Huellas de Arte (Footprints of Art) foundation, under the auspices of the Church of Sweden.[1] In this participatory action research (PAR), members of the Huellas de Arte read the story about the rape of Princess Tamar (2 Samuel 13:1–22).[2] The text was read by twenty members of the organization; eight women and four men who participated in four monthly work sessions. They were in the company of a group made up of six theologians and a psychologist.

---

1. The research project (ID 00006554) was developed from July 2014 and December 2016, within the framework of the activities of the "Didaskalia" Theological Teaching and Research Team.

2. The terms of reference of the Church of Sweden's convocation stipulated that research should be carried out in accordance with the Participatory Action Research (PAR) approach.

The chapter has four parts. The first part presents the methodological framework, which demonstrates the affinity and complementarity between the community experience of the Contextual Reading of the Bible (CRB) and the methodology of PAR. The second part describes the composition, history, and work of the Huellas de Arte, as well as the overcoming of initial obstacles that some of its members faced regarding the use of biblical texts as tools for indoctrination. The third part deals with the narrative of the rape of Princess Tamar and her self-stigmatization due to the humiliation she was subjected to (2 Samuel 13:1–22). There is also a reference to the origin of the Tamar Campaign against sexual and gender-based violence in some African countries. The fourth part presents the results of the interpretation of the biblical text by the members of the Huellas de Arte foundation in the framework of the CRB. At the end of the chapter, some general observations from this experience are made about gender-based violence.

Contextual Reading of the Bible and Participatory Action Research

The Contextual Reading of the Bible (CRB) is a process of action-reflection used by some communities to interpret biblical texts through real-life experiences. In this way, the communities critically appropriate their reality and transform it in a liberating way. It is a process in which biblical studies converge with community practices to improve the living conditions of the readers of sacred texts. As Carlos Dreher, of the Center for biblical Studies (CEBI) of Brazil, puts it, "God wants a better life for the people. So may the Bible speak to you in this life. Consequently, it is necessary to know life before reading any text. From life, we move towards the Bible, wherein we seek the Word that best illuminates our life situation. Then we come back to life to transform it."[3]

The purpose of transforming reality makes the contextual reading of biblical texts a tool of liberation because the texts reveal to people new possible worlds. When the texts are interpreted from the world of people, they unfold unpublished worlds before their readers. In this sense, Paul Ricoeur understood the revealed character of the Sacred Scriptures as authentic revelations. "If the Bible can be called revealed, the same should be said of the *thing* that it says; of the new *being* that it deploys. I would dare then to say that the Bible is revealed in the same way that the new being that is

---

3. Dreher, *The Walk to Emmaus*, 26.

revealed becomes the *revealer* with respect to the world, to the complete reality, including my existence and my history."[4]

Biblical texts are much more than objects of study. In fact, they are a source of life for those who are willing to let themselves be questioned by them. The interpretation of the sacred texts brings new life to communities by unfolding their liberating spirit. This is what is meant when it is affirmed that "the Gospel lives in its interpretations and transcends them."[5] This transcendental expansion of sacred texts has allowed people to act in every moment throughout history, providing an inexhaustible reserve of sense and meaning each time they are read through the lived realities of different communities. As José Severino Croatto explains of the operative reality of the word: It "opens up to our own experiences, providing a key to interpretation. . . . But it is not present simply because we read it now, in our context, but above all, because it is archetypal and paradigmatic, and as such, it serves as a model to interpret our own reality."[6]

In the CRB approach, life comes first, and then the word that permits it to be interpreted. Carlos Mesters explains: "Indeed, the Bible was not the first book that God wrote for us, nor the most important. The first book . . . are the facts, events, history, everything that exists and happens in the life of the people. It is the reality that surrounds us."[7] The experience of reading a biblical text within its vital world allows communities to consume the life of the text and thereby, to change their reality, so the role of theologians and biblical scholars who participate in the contextual reading of a biblical text should be limited to companionship in the transformation process.

This accompaniment is a challenge for academics, as some are accustomed to directing the reflection of communities with their professional knowledge. In CRB, theologians and biblical scholars must not only recognize the legitimacy of the communities' popular knowledge, but also, they must accept that this knowledge is located at the same hierarchical level as their specialized knowledge, acquired throughout many years of study and work. That is the necessary condition for undertaking a genuinely liberating journey: to walk as peers. This is explained by Gerald West, of the Ujamaa Centre at the University of KwaZulu-Natal: "At the center of a liberating hermeneutics is the relationship between the Biblical scholars (or

4. Ricœur, *Du texte à l' action*, 141–42.
5. López, *La evangelización*, 50.
6. Croatto, *Hermenéutica práctica*, 16.
7. Mesters, *Flor sin defensa*, 28.

theologians) and the common Christian" reader "of a poor and marginalized community."[8]

This relationship is doubly liberating for academics: on a moral and intellectual level. In the end, they will not only have freed themselves from the domination of their own interests, through their commitment to the struggle for the rights of marginalized groups and popular communities, but they will also have freed themselves from the limitations of a purely theoretical and speculative knowledge of revelation. Reality is not the only thing that ends up being transformed. In the relationship with the community, there is also a transformation of those who accompany the emancipatory process of the community.

CRB is based on seeing, judging, and acting. It was developed in Belgium by Monsignor Joseph Cardijn when he worked with the Catholic Working Youth in the 1930s. This method, which seeks to overcome the distance between faith and life, was taken up four decades later by Liberation Theology. In the logic of seeing, judging and acting, we begin from reality to understand it. We go to the biblical texts to value it, and we return to reality to transform it. This is what Clodovis Boff says about the method of Liberation Theology: "In liberation theology, there are three main mediations: socio-analytic mediation, hermeneutical mediation, and practical mediation."[9]

In the contextual reading of biblical texts, corresponding to hermeneutical mediation in this scheme, we start from a spontaneous reflection at the level of community consciousness, then we pass through the level of critical consciousness by generating questions that allow us to go deeper into the text, and then we return to the level of community consciousness.[10] The days dedicated to contextual biblical studies begin with the general perception that the readers have of the subject of the text. From their own contextual perspective, the participants then critically delve into the literary and historical aspects of the text; they do this through careful reading, guided by questions formulated by the companions and by the community itself.[11] Then the consciousness of the community appears again before the contextual reality to transform it according to the new critical interpretation of the text.

8. West, "Do Two Walk Together?" 437.
9. Boff, "Epistemología y método de la teología de la liberación," 101.
10. West, "Do Two Walk Together?" 446–48.
11. West, "Contribution of Tamar's Story," 184–200.

The CRB process responds to the community's own agenda, or that of the group of readers, because it is prioritized above the agenda of those who serve as companions. It is a community experience, in which the subjects face problems in their real lives in the light of the biblical texts. The intention to transform reality and the central role of the group or the community makes this way of reading the Bible compatible with PAR.

PAR privileges the active participation of communities and is based on the knowledge they have about their reality. The method aims to promote justice through the very agency of social groups and vulnerable communities. The main purpose of PAR is the transformation of human living conditions, as proposed by the Colombian sociologist Orlando Fals, based on the "interests of the working and peasant classes, or other groups that have been maintained under the law of silence."[12] As in CRB, in PAR, the contributions made by the academics based on their specialized knowledge are no more important than the contributions made by the communities based on their popular wisdom.

According to Fals, the participants in PAR are considered "as people connected to each other by feelings, rules, and attitudes, with diverse opinions and experiences that can be taken into account."[13] The groups of professionals and communities take an active part in the research design together, developing its phases and using the results to change their reality. A PAR process must begin with an initial phase of connection between communities and academics, to deal with the participatory definition of the problem, the joint collection of information, and the shared analysis of the data obtained, as well as the collaborative planning of the strategies of intervention in the reality that it seeks to transform.

In PAR, mutual knowledge begins to encourage trust between the community members and the research team. This first phase can take several months, as time is necessary for generating the bonds that make possible joint work framed by symmetrical relations of power. Then, we proceed to identify a situation that affects the community and can be transformed into research. It is a dimension of reality that must be represented then as a problem of departing from reality, as proposed in the logic of seeing, judging, and acting.

Once the problem (which, in the case of Huellas de Arte, was the sustainability of the organization; due to the concentration of leadership

12. Fals, "La ciencia y el pueblo," 71.
13. Fals, "La ciencia y el pueblo," 160.

in two of the members of the organization and the lack of economic resources), the CRB was developed from 2 Samuel 13:1–22. The biblical text was addressed by generating questions[14] that allowed the participants to place themselves at the level of critical awareness and to situate themselves vis-à-vis their own reality, in relation to the stigma associated with their health condition and sexual violence. Through the experience of CRB, the members of Huellas de Arte acquired their own resources to enhance their political advocacy and their work on one of the fronts of action of the organization, namely educating women about human, sexual, and reproductive rights.

The four sessions devoted to contextual biblical study were recorded. Their transcriptions were then subjected to axial coding, as proposed by Anselm Strauss and Juliet Corbin, with the purpose of developing a grounded theory: "Axial coding is the act of relating categories to subcategories, following the lines of their properties and dimensions."[15] The analysis was validated by the members of Huellas de Arte, and this validation helped them to reconstruct their reality, affected by stigmatization and sexual violence. In the validation process of the codes and categories obtained from their own affirmations, the participants found specific ways to transform this reality. In the end, the members of the organization assumed new commitments, and a productive project was proposed to guarantee the sustainability of the foundation.

This was the participatory methodological framework that helped the members of Huellas de Arte to appropriate their reality with the aim of transforming it. With their own interpretation of the story of Princess Tamar (2 Samuel 13:1–22), CRB allowed them to recognize themselves in

---

14. These included: What is this text about? Who are the characters in the narrative? What do they do? What do they feel? With which characters of the story do they identify? What role does each of the male characters play in Tamar's rape? What allows Amnon to act in accordance with his sick love? According to Tamar, what should a man be like? What kind of man is Amnon? What does Tamar say and do in the different parts of the story? What are Amnon's reactions to Tamar's responses? What is Amnon's behavior after he raped Tamar? What is the relationship between Tamar's gestures at the end of the story and the stigma of those living with HIV? Do you know cases like Tamar's? Can you share those stories with the group? What possibilities and resources do women who have been victims of sexual violence have? What could Huellas de Arte do in the face of events such as those recounted in Tamar's story and those that have been told by the members of the group through their stories? How have they felt during the unfolding of this activity?

15. Strauss and Corbin, *Bases de la investigación cualitativa*, 135.

the narrative and to project new worlds in their fight against stigmatization and sexual violence.

The Huellas de Arte Foundation

The Huellas de Arte Foundation is an organization made up of people from popular sectors, who live and coexist with HIV. Most of them are women, but recently some men have joined. Due to social prejudices and lack of information about the transmission of the virus, their health condition makes them subject to stigmatization and consequent social discrimination. When beginning the CRB experience, the organization consisted of approximately 30 people, of whom 20 regularly participated in the monthly meetings: 16 women and four men.

In the Colombian imagination, those who contract HIV are believed to have led a life of sexual promiscuity or to have used psychoactive substances intravenously. However, most of the members of Huellas de Arte are homemakers who have been infected by their partners, on whom they have been economically dependent for many years.

The women who are part of the Foundation constitute a minority among the people living with HIV/AIDS (PLWHA). In addition to being in contexts not recognized as particularly vulnerable, in Colombia, the prevalence of infection among women is very low compared to men. According to the Ministry of Health and Social Protection, in 2011, 73.1 percent of the people infected were men, and 26.9 percent were women.[16] In accordance with these percentages, the health system has focused its efforts on the care of population segments with higher prevalence, such as men who have sex with men.[17]

At the end of 2009, approximately 17,000[18] women were living with the virus, a significantly large population beyond the proportional percentages. However, women living with HIV outside contexts recognized as highly vulnerable do not constitute a particular group of interest for public health care policies.

Since its inception in 2002, Huellas de Arte has been concerned with influencing the formulation, implementation, and evaluation of public policies to promote the rights of women living with and coexisting with the virus. Using a different and gendered perspective, the foundation has sought

16. Ministerio de Salud y Protección Social, 18.
17. Ministerio de Salud y Protección Social, 19.
18. Ávila, "¿Qué está pasando con el Sida en Colombia?"

greater equity for women in access to paid work and health services. It has also fought for the prevention of the virus. Through the exercise of citizen oversight, it has made some significant achievements, such as the construction of the *Methodological Guide for Strengthening the Political Impact of the National Network of Popular Women Weaving Life* (*Guía Metodológica para el Fortalecimiento y la Incidencia Política de la Red Nacional de Mujeres Populares Tejiendo Vida*), and the explicit inclusion of women as a population group in the *National Plan of Response to STDs/HIV/AIDS 2014–2017*.

The work of Huellas de Arte is guided by the values of respect, resilience, and solidarity. The foundation has four fields of action: the accompaniment of women who have recently received the diagnosis; the training of women in human, sexual, and reproductive rights; the training of leaders and activists; and the search for economic resources for the sustainability of the organization.

Organizations such as Huellas de Arte still face many challenges in supporting women living with HIV/AIDS in Colombia appropriating what it means to be a subject of rights. The stigmatization of these women because of their health status often results in their resigned acceptance of the curtailing of their fundamental rights, particularly their sexual and reproductive rights. This limitation is often promoted by health professionals, health authorities, and church institutions.

Through popular education, the foundation has sought to make women increasingly aware of their rights and their duty to exercise them. The emancipatory work of the foundation allows women to overcome the victimization and guilt that often accompany their diagnosis. Being diagnosed as HIV positive has been, for these people, one of the most challenging experiences of their lives. In addition to the immediate association that is usually established between HIV, AIDS, and death, they are surrounded by intense feelings of shame and social fear.

The sexism that permeates the structures of Colombian society and its cultural practices make many women consider themselves dependent on men, because of the role of men as providers of economic resources and sustenance for their families. For this reason, the foundation has also worked to prepare its members to participate in productive projects related to the manufacture of candles and dolls with Christmas motifs. The name "Huellas de Arte" derives from this activity, through which some women have striven to obtain economic resources in order to achieve financial independence from those who infected them with the virus, and who, in some cases, used sexual violence against them. In the research process, it became evident that these projects could be beneficial and liberating for these women. It was therefore determined that they would also undertake a project of manufacturing and commercializing sleepwear.

In addition to the background of the Tamar Campaign against sexual and gender-based violence in specific African countries, the Tamar narrative was chosen as the object of a CRB in this group because of social inequity based on gender and stigmatization of health status. However, during the research project, it became evident that some women in the organization had also been victims of sexual violence, as in the story about the princess of the House of David. This observation gave the experience of CRB a greater therapeutic and emancipatory value than initially anticipated.

The initial mistrust of a group of male theologians belonging to the Catholic Church, one of the institutions that has blamed and stigmatized these women for their health condition, was gradually dispelled by the joint work of the first four monthly meetings aimed at building mutual trust. Without a doubt, having the support of a psychologist on the research team helped establish a bridge that favored confidence building. At the end of the first semester of the process, the members of the organization perceived the group of theologians and biblical scholars as peers with whom they had established symmetrical relationships, not as proselytizing Christians interested in their indoctrination. At that time, the participants of Huellas de Arte felt secure enough to share with them the contextual reading of the biblical narrative.

Except for one case, the participants had no experience in communal Bible reading. In the beginning, they associated the sacred texts with indoctrination aimed at the conversion of customs, but their expectations of the contextual reading of the Tamar narrative progressively grew among them, which would continue during the second semester.

Profound cultural transformations are necessary for HIV-infected women to be free, not only from the discrimination associated with stigmatization for their health status but also from the sexual violence that many have experienced.

The Rape of Princess Tamar
and Her Self-Stigmatization in 2 Samuel 13:1–22

This section of the Second Book of Samuel is closely related to the experiences of stigmatization endured by the members of the Huellas de Arte

Foundation, as well as to the sexual violence to which some of its members have been subjected. It includes a narrative that introduces the struggle between Amnon and Absalom for their father's throne, the throne of David. The story of the rape of Princess Tamar is a tragedy that gives rise to a fratricidal struggle that determined the political course of the house of David and the fate of Israel.

From the beginning of history, the condition of women was a relationship of dependence on men. The presentation of the princess is as follows: "David's son Absalom had a very beautiful sister whose name was; and David's son Amnon fell in love with her" (v. 1). Although all-male violence falls upon this beautiful young woman, Tamar is a secondary character in the narrative. However, in the CRB experience, the princess was the center of attention for the members of Huellas de Arte.

Prisoner of his sickly love for Tamar, and following the advice of his cunning cousin Jonadab, Amnon pretends to be sick and has David send Tamar to prepare food to serve to him: "Amnon went to bed and pretended to be sick. The King went in to see him, and Amnon said to him, 'Let my sister Tamar come and make a couple of cakes in my sight, so that I may eat from her hand.'" (v. 6).

This is a clear conspiracy plotted by the male characters against Princess Tamar, who is the only person who presents God's mercy in the narrative. Indeed, she willingly cares for her brother's well-being. She, therefore, obeys the King's order, despite the risk involved,[19] and goes to Amnon's house to prepare and give him the food that will return him to health. This last aspect of the narrative is important in the day's readings, because of the analogy with the situation of so many women who care for men. This situation shows the contrast of the violence, which is often sexual violence, that men commit against them. Once at Amnon's house, while trying to help him regain his health, the princess is taken by force and raped: "But he would not listen to her; and being stronger than she, he forced her and lay with her" (v. 14).

Amnon's house was a place where the safety of the princess was at risk. Perhaps this was known to David, who sent the order for the Princess to go there and prepare food for his supposedly sick brother. The complicity of David, who was angry for what was done to Tamar but did nothing to prevent it and who did not admonish Amnon afterward (v. 21), can be explained by what the King had done before when he fell in love with

19. Fokkelman, *Narrative Art and Poetry in the Books of Samuel*, 103.

Bathsheba. The King took her by force, slept with her, and then planned the death of her husband (2 Samuel 11:2–17).

As if a premonition, once at her brother's house and before his watchful gaze, Tamar had prepared some heart-shaped doughnuts. This erotic connotation to the food, as well as the process of preparing fried food before Amnon's eyes, is underlined by commentators such as Arnold Andersson.[20] Other commentators, such as Elaine Neuenfeldt, demonstrate that the form and preparation of food in this narrative may be related to rituals of offering and divination to cure males of impotence.[21]

Immediately after the rape, Amnon's alleged love for Tamar (2 Samuel 13:4) became hatred of her: "Then Amnon was seized with a very great loathing for her; indeed, his loathing was even greater than the lust he had felt for her" (v. 15a). Amnon said to her, "Get out!" (v.15b), and then he called his servant and said to him, "Put this woman out of my presence and bolt the door after her" (v.17b). According to Jan Fokkelman, the young princess witnessed Amnon's inhumanity, and this witnessing makes him afraid. While he once wanted to become close to Tamar, now he wants her far away and he throws her out of his house. He then locks the door to avoid a new confrontation should she return.[22]

When Tamar becomes aware of Amnon's intentions to rape her, she confronts him wisely. She demonstrates the terrible consequences that rape would bring for both of them, and proposes a solution: "She answered him, 'No, my brother, do not force me; for such a thing is not done in Israel; do not do anything so vile! As for me, where could I carry my shame? And as for you, you would be as one of the scoundrels in Israel. Now therefore, I beg you, speak to the king; for he will not withhold me from you'" (vv. 12–14). With the same wisdom, Tamar reacts to Amnon's order to leave his house: "But she said to him, 'No, my brother; for this wrong in sending me away is greater than the other that you did to me'" (v. 16a). Despite the subordination of women in the cultural context of the story, the story highlights the Princess' brave and intelligent reaction to her brother's deplorable intentions.

The way Tamar is presented at the beginning of the narrative, as Absalom's sister, indicates that this double humiliation is inflicted not only on the Princess, but also on Absalom's house. The contrast between the initial

20. Andersson, 2 Samuel, 172.

21. Neuenfeldt, "Sexual Violence and Power."

22. Fokkelman, Narrative Art and Poetry in the Books of Samuel, 108.

strong attraction to Tamar and the subsequent hatred felt towards her is not only a change in Amnon's feelings but evidence of the hatred between his and Absalom's houses. At the end of the narrative, itreads: "But Absalom spoke to Amnon neither good nor bad; for Absalom hated Amnon, because he had raped his sister Tamar" (v. 22). Later, in the next section of the Second Book of Samuel, two years later, Absalom takes revenge and kills his brother (vv. 23–29).

Although Absalom allowed Tamar to live in his home after being a victim of Amnon's sexual violence, initiated by Jonadab with the collaboration of David, Absalom'srole in the event makes his complicity evident. In meeting the Princess after the rape, his words not only confirm his knowledge of what had happened but also impose silence on Tamar, because her victimizer belongs to the royal family: "Her brother Absalom said to her, 'Has Amnon your brother been with you? Be quiet for now, my sister; he is your brother; do not take this to heart.' So Tamar remained, a desolate woman, in her brother Absalom's house" (v. 20).

After the double vexation to which she has been subjected, Tamar demonstrates her humiliation in public. As she walks down the street, she screams with her hands on her head in an expression of pain.[23] This may be a cry for help. For, according to commentators such as Graeme Auld, the text indicates she screams further.[24] Tearing the sleeves of the tunic that she had worn when she was a virgin, and putting ash on her head, like soldiers who have been defeated in war (v. 19), are related to her new and unhappy condition.

Tamar seems to stigmatize herself after being raped by Amnon and thrown out of her house. Due to the sexual violence she was subjected to by her brother, with the complicity of the other male members of her family, this young woman could not live her sexuality as she should have. Tamar is condemned to live alone, a terrible fate for a woman in that cultural context. She will not marry any man, nor will she have any offspring, and the Bible will no longer mention her.

In addition to Tamar's reaction to her victimization, this terrible narrative was chosen for this CRB experience because of the common background of women who have experienced similar violence. In South Africa, a contextual reading of this story gave rise to the Tamar Campaign to break the silence of sexual and gender-based violence. In 1996, the Institute for

23. Fokkelman, *Narrative Art and Poetry in the Books of Samuel*, 110.
24. Auld, *I and II Samuel: A Commentary*, 475.

Biblical Study and the Ministerial Worker project, in cooperation with the Ujamaa Centre, organized the international workshop, "Women and the Bible in South Africa."[25] One of the working themes of this workshop was "Woman and Violence," for which the text 2 Samuel 13:1–22 was chosen, and was then the object of CRB.

After this workshop, several local communities invited researchers from the Ujamaa Centre to conduct other contextual biblical studies of the same story. In one such study, which took place in Hammarsdale,[26] a group of young women challenged the members of the Centre, asking what other resources they could offer them "to break the chains of silence . . . the result was the birth of 'The Tamar Campaign.'"[27]

That campaign began in South Africa in 2000, thanks to the work of Gerald West, Phumzile Zondi-Mabizela, Futhi Ntshingila, and Sarojini Nadar. Within a few years, it had spread to Kenya, Zambia, Cameroon, Nigeria, and Angola. As part of the Tamar Campaign, a seminar was held in Kenya from March 2 to March 4, 2005, to raise critical awareness of violence against children and women, particularly sexual violence to women's bodies.[28]

The work of the Tamar Campaign has as its permanent foundation the narration of the violence suffered by the young Princess, who was brave and did not remain silent after her rape.[29] The campaign seeks to provide information on gender-based violence, to stand with victims, and offer training to the male population, grounded in compassion and the promotion of justice. In recent years, the campaign has also involved other issues related to economic justice and the scourge of HIV/AIDS.

This story about the Princess who, after being a victim of sexual violence, confronted her aggressor and broke the silence they wanted to impose on herencouraged twenty members of Huellas de Arte to review their own experiences of stigmatization and sexual violence. The identification with Tamar's humiliation and self-stigmatization allowed the participants to reconstruct and transform their own reality, through a careful, critical, and liberating reading of this biblical text.

---

25. West and Zondi-Mazibela, "Bible Story that Became a Campaign."
26. West and Zondi-Mazibela, "Bible Story that Became a Campaign," 9.
27. West, "Contribution of Tamar's Story," 186.
28. Khabure, "Tamar Campaign Seminar."
29. West, "Contribution of Tamar's Story."

Contextual Reading of 2 Samuel 13:1–22 by Huellas de Arte

In addition to the restructuring of Huellas de Arte to develop the individual and collective capacities of its members and undertake a new productive project, a double response to the main problem identified through participatory action research (PAR), the contextual reading of the biblical narrative about Tamar enabled the members of the organization to take ownership of their reality, critically situate themselves before it, and find new means to transform it. To facilitate participation and create a more trusting environment, the group of twenty participants was divided into three smaller groups: two women's groups (groups 1 and 2) and one men's group (group 3).

The critical appropriation of their lives and texts, made by the participants during the CRB experience, can be seen in the results presented in this section on four topics: (a) male power and women's fear; (b) women's exercise of sexuality and women's improved control over their own bodies; (c) women's sexual violence and silence; and (d) the relationship between diagnosis, social stigmatization, and self-stigmatization.[30]

Male Power and Women's Fear

The initial question, "What is the text about?" was proposed at the beginning of all the sessions devoted to the interpretation of the biblical narrative, after a celebratory moment when the text was read out loud to all those present. Power often appeared as the central theme of the story: "That sexual abuse, like all sexual abuse, is not perpetrated for pleasure but to exercise power, to increase the power I have."[31]

Indeed, among the topics covered by the text, the rape of Tamar, as an expression of masculine power not limited to physical force stood out: "A rape mediated by the abuse of power, in all senses; by hierarchical power, but also by the power of force . . . normally men use the power of force, which is often a physical power, but also economic power when women depend on them."[32]

Not infrequently, the power of men creates fear in women, as one of the participants pointed out in the fear that her ex-husband still produces

30. Some of the data presented here are also in López, "Reading 2 Sam 13:1–22."
31. Group 2. April 12, 2015.
32. Group 1. April 12, 2015.

in her: "Even today, I see him, and I feel fear."[33] Hence, the figure of Tamar, a woman capable of confronting her aggressor in a sexist and patriarchal society, has special importance. This was the experience of the participants in this CRB, who found in the attitude of the princess a new motivation for overcoming the dominion of male power in their own lives.

This narrative has a strong relationship with the lives of the women who belong to the organization. In sexist and patriarchal societies, the will of men takes precedence over the needs of women. Sexual violence is a reality today, even in married life. In the words of one participant: "There is sexual violence in marriages. If he wants to, he wants to. As women, we feel obliged to say, 'he is my husband, therefore if he touches me, I must do it.'"[34]

The fear that many women have of male power is well-founded, as reflected in the following testimony of one participant: "My ex-husband committed many abuses against me. He did many things, and I was very afraid of him; it was a terrible fear. They (my husband and his family) had a lot of money and threatened to take away my children."[35] This is just one example of how domestic violence relies on the economic and political power that men hold in sexist societies.

Faced with the possibility of marriage between Amnon and Tamar, one of the women said: "She had the conditions and could have done well, but it was clear to her that she was an object of desire, and he only wanted her to satisfy a purely sexual pleasure because he was attracted by her beauty."[36] However, the solution proposed by Tamar to the threat of being raped by her brother did not satisfy all of the participants, because, as one of them said, "the fact that she has to accept and say 'no, come on, stay with me,' that nothing has happened here, is very thought-provoking."[37]

This dissatisfaction can be seen as the origin of judgment regarding what a woman is willing to accept from others. Already in one of the first sessions dedicated to the detailed reading of the biblical story, one of the participants said: "Many women accept that their partners sexually abuse them because, if they are kicked out, or if they leave, they have nowhere to go."[38]

33. Group 1. April 12, 2015.

34. Group 1. April 12, 2015.

35. Group 1. April 12, 2015.

36. Group 1. April 12, 2015.

37. Group 2. April 12, 2015.

38. Group 2. February 8, 2015.

According to the readers of the story, Tamar is the victim of a plot conceived by Amnon and Jonadab, who have the complicity of David and Absalom. The power of the men in the narrative produces fear in the young woman, as one participant stated: "For fear of what the King might say . . . she preferred to remain under Amnon's dominion."[39] The Princess has no support, not even that of her father, whose excessive tolerance makes him an accomplice to the rapist: "Even his father, who was the person responsible for reprimanding and punishing, did not do so."[40]

All the men in the narrative have power, but Amnon stands out among them: "As he was her brother, she allowed him to do everything against her; there was no one to defend her."[41] About this, one of the participants said, "In reality, Tamar's chances were minimal, and in the end, she had to take all the blame because of this mental degenerate."[42]

The experience of CRB was also challenging for the male members of Huellas de Arte, because it helped them to become aware of how difficult it is to "put themselves in the situation of the other and, even more so, in the situation of the opposite sex, because their life experiences are so different."[43] In this sense, it was a great help to have assigned to them the role of Tamar during a dramatization of the narration, which was done in one of the first encounters. On that occasion, they said, "Of course, what our female colleagues say is true. One never puts oneself in the role of a woman; but once you try to imagine it for yourself, then your thinking changes. It feels different."[44]

The Exercise of Sexuality and Women's Control over Their Own Bodies

According to the participants in the contextual reading of this biblical narrative, the text clearly demonstrates the denial of female sexuality and women's control of their own bodies. Already during the first days reading of the text, this became evident: "It's what they always say: 'The woman's body is not even her own.'"[45]

---

39. Group 1. April 12, 2015.
40. Group 1. April 12, 2015.
41. Group 1. April 12, 2015.
42. Group 1. April 12, 2015.
43. Group 1. April 12, 2015.
44. Group 3. March 8, 2015.
45. Group 3. March 8, 2015.

For some of the readers of the Tamar story, a woman's control of her own body is a key concept in capturing the meaning of the narrative. At that time, and even today, the woman's body is seen instrumentally as a source of pleasure for the man, as a means to obtain offspring, or simply as a means to maintain domestic life: "The woman's body has always been managed by the man. Yes, in terms of being a sexual object; but, in other instances, it is also for washing, ironing, cooking, and doing the housework."[46]

A woman's body is not recognized as her own domain, but as an instrument of domination of others over them: that is "our castration . . . we were made to procreate."[47] One of the participants said about this instrumental evaluation of the woman's body, "there is no recognition of the woman, only as a means of reproduction, to maintain the species, as a sexual object . . . in the house the woman should not have any pleasure because she is only there for reproduction."[48]

Identifying with the victim of the plan conceived and carried out by the men of the royal family, one of the participants stated, "my body has never been my own. In this case, she [Tamar] said, 'my body belongs to my father.'"[49] This reality, which many young women must endure in patriarchal societies, was perceived by the participants from the very beginning of the CRB: "[the woman] must take care of her virginity and give it to whomever her father says. He decides who she is going to marry or who she is going to sleep with, to whom she is going to give her virginity."[50]

For some of the participants, the medicalization of their condition has also served as a social control mechanism over their sexuality. This has been a limiting factor in their sexual and reproductive rights. "Women who live with HIV are even deprived of reproduction. When the doctor finds out that the lady is pregnant, he has no hesitation in saying to her: 'How irresponsible you are!' . . . I hope you don't have a sexual life because you are irresponsible if you do."[51]

The work that Huellas de Arte does to make women aware of their sexual rights was evident during the contextual reading of the narrative, when one of them said, "I am sure that sexuality is directly associated with

46. Group 1. April 12, 2015.
47. Group 2. April 12, 2015.
48. Group 1. April 12, 2015.
49. Group 2. April 12, 2015.
50. Group 2. February 8, 2015.
51. Group 2. April 12, 2015.

the exercise of autonomy because if I am sexually happy, I am happy in everything and feel confident in myself."[52] The history of Tamar vindicates the struggle of Huellas de Arte for the sexual and reproductive rights of women: "Our sexuality has always been subordinated to others, to procreation . . . Only now we want to have our sexuality complete, placidly, healthily . . . we have fought, and we have to keep fighting."[53]

There is still much that organizations like this must do in Colombia, so that women can exercise their sexuality autonomously. A great institutional and social effort is required so that many women may break their silence and become free from the sexual violence to which they have been subjected.

Sexual Violence and Women's Silence

During this CRB experience, it became evident that some of the participants had been victims of sexual violence. Their testimonies were overwhelming, especially when they referred to the sexual abuse of children by their own family members. Some of the stories told by the participants included re-victimization by families, authorities, and health workers.

In addition to violence, some of these victims had been blamed for the rape and had suffered physical violence from their own families because of the violence against them: "With my body completely bruised by my mother's blows, I had to explain (to the forensic authorities) that I had been beaten by my own mother and not by my rapist,"[54] said one participant after recounting her ordeal.

According to some of the participants who had been abused, "it's harder to endure being labelled than to endure the violation itself."[55] It is not easy to face re-victimization by the authorities, not least of all when the complaint is made. "You must justify your condition as a victim. That is terrible. It is worse than rape itself. As Tamar said, it is a worse evil than rape itself, having to justify yourself before the state and its justice for being a victim."[56]

The authorities often employ structural violence, as reflected in the testimony that one of the participants shared with her group: "I have the

52. Group 2. April 12, 2015.
53. Group 2. May 31, 2015.
54. Group 2. May 31, 2015.
55. Group 2. May 31, 2015.
56. Group 2. May 31, 2015.

record because I went to the police, but they only made a few tests in which I felt even more abused."[57] The sexism of Colombian culture makes it even more difficult to denounce sexual violence, as one of the participants points out when she recalls a terrible experience of youth lived years ago: "When I denounced the father of my daughters, the lady told me 'you must go home to clean up and serve your husband.' That happened to me thirty years ago, I had the signs of the blows on my face . . . I told myself 'he hits me, he rapes me . . . I need help' . . . I was seventeen years old then and already had two girls."[58]

The biblical story led women who had experienced sexual violence to identify with the courageous figure of Tamar because during their lives, they had to remain silent about terrible things to avoid social disapproval. The critical and profound interpretation of the biblical story then served as an expression of the need to be vocal in the face of the sexual abuses to which they and other women have been subjected.

The humiliations suffered by Tamar are repeated in the daily lives of many women who submit to their partners due to economic and cultural pressures. As stated by one of the participants:

> A woman must accept it when her husband arrives drunk and sexually abuses her. She is silent because it is she who is responsible for the family. Then he hits me, rapes me, sexually abuses me, even in front of the children, and I simply remain silent, because I was taught that I have to keep my home. I must keep my title of "Mrs."[59]

In many cases of sexual violence, women are blamed for the perpetrators' actions. As one participant put it: "People are not going to blame the perpetrator; however, women do not have the status of victims, so they are often considered the 'provocative cause' of it. We're almost seen as the actors, and we're blamed for what happens to us."[60]

This was corroborated by the group of men who participated in the CRB experience, who referred to a well-known case that occurred some years ago in a famous restaurant near Bogotá: "As has happened, for example, in the case of the girl from 'Andrés Carne de Res,' they raped her, and she denounced it. There and then they said: 'No, but sister, if you were

57. Group 1. April 12, 2015.
58. Group 2. May 31, 2015.
59. Group 2. April 12, 2015.
60. Group 1. April 12, 2015.

in a miniskirt, then how are they not going to rape you? Shut up then and say nothing.'"[61]

Although there are laws prohibiting sexual violence, in addition to widespread impunity, there is also complicity in families. Establishing a clear relationship between current daily life and Tamar's case, one woman said: "'There are still brothers who rape their sisters, and also parents who know it. In order to avoid comments or scandals in the family, everything is kept quiet. It is forbidden to talk about the subject."[62]

The CRB allowed some participants to discuss the gap between the private sphere of their family lives and the image they must project in the public sphere. Breaking the silence about sexual violence in one's own home is a necessity, even though it affects the image of their partners, who are the perpetrators of the sexual violence they suffer:

> "Don't wash your dirty linen in public!" so the idea is to manage the public and the private. In private, they can beat me. Others can do whatever they want to me, but this happens in private. Nobody knows it because if it is revealed in public, the image of that terrible person deteriorates. . . . In private, they can "beat me, kick me, rape me"; and I must fulfill my matrimonial duties, which are not only to wash, iron, or cook, but also to be ready when my man decides he wants me.[63]

Silence was a major theme in the participants' conversations, not only in the face of sexual violence and sexual abuse but also in relation to their experiences of structural and cultural violence vis-à-vis HIV. They must keep their diagnosis secret in order to avoid being blamed and stigmatized.

The Relationship Among Diagnosis, Stigmatization, and Self-Stigmatization

Regarding the relationship between Tamar's gestures at the end of the story and the reality of those living with HIV, the participants spoke about their fear of letting others know about their health status. One of the women from the organization stated: "When I was informed about my diagnosis, I thought about what might happen to me and what my colleagues might

---

61. Group 3. May 31, 2015.
62. Group 1. April 12, 2015.
63. Group 1. April 12, 2015.

think. If I approached them, they might reject me."[64] There is a strong concern among the participants regarding their working conditions: "What are my co-workers going to do? They are going to say, 'She shared with me. I'm afraid she infected me.'"[65]

Most people in Colombia do not have sufficient information about the virus: "Everything is associated with AIDS and death. It's a very complex issue, and that's why discrimination is very strong."[66] One of the participants, from a rural area, shared a negative experience: "In a small town, it is very difficult because people have no idea what the infection is . . . I knew the case of a young man in a village, he had HIV, and when the paramilitaries found out, they made him 'disappear.'"[67]

In the case of some women, the fear stems not only from the consequences for themselves but also for their children. This is evident in the following testimony:

> I think that like Tamar, people with HIV are told we must be silent. What Absalom said to Tamar. . . . At the end, he says that Tamar was heartbroken. . . . In the case of women, we have to think that we have behind us "a little tail that can be stepped on," our children. I wouldn't have any problem if it came to light, but I think about the discrimination towards them. . . . My children know about my diagnosis, but they also know that they must remain silent.[68]

According to some participants, despite the fear of the stigma associated with the rape she was subjected to, and without any support, Tamar resisted remaining silent. Unlike the young woman in the biblical story, they now have the support of Huellas de Arte, a foundation that works to support people who are diagnosed as HIV-positive. This is very important assistance because they have a support network and a safe place to break the silence about their health condition: "Tamar herself tore her cloak . . . that's what happens with HIV . . . She went out and all the people in the village realized it."[69]

According to the biblical account, "Tamar threw ashes on her head, tore the long-sleeved tunic she was wearing, put her hands on her head, and

---

64. Group 1. April 12, 2015.

65. Group 1. April 12, 2015.

66. Group 1. April 12, 2015.

67. Group 1. April 12, 2015.

68. Group 2, May 31, 2015.

69. Group 2, May 31, 2015.

shouted as she walked" (v. 19). This reminded some participants of their feelings at the precise moment they were diagnosed by healthcare professionals. They were alone in front of a desk, without any advice after the examination. This was just one more manifestation of the structural violence that leads to self-stigmatization: "You beat yourself up . . . you want to run away, scream and cry . . . one feels that the earth is swallowing you up . . . I had to face the situation for myself, alone like poor Tamar."[70]

Absalom's question to Tamar, "Has your stepbrother Amnon been with you?" (v. 20) was associated by some readers with other people's curiosity, including health service officials, about the cause of their infection. Such an inquiry is often a response to prejudices about the virus in relation to sexual promiscuity or the intravenous use of psychoactive substances.

The cultural violence suffered by women in a sexist society is compounded by prejudices about contagion. One respondent stated, "The greatest fear of a person living with HIV of revealing their diagnosis is not associated with people fearing that I will pass on the infection, but with that value judgment they make about my sexual behavior."[71]

These prejudices have a profound impact on family relationships, as making the diagnosis public can lead to a double humiliation, like that suffered by Tamar. This is how one of the participants puts it: "One is not only discriminated against by society. When the family knows you're like this, they don't speak to you again. The story is similar to what one is living through at the present time. Everything has to be kept quiet. Let no one know, otherwise, you are discriminated against or kicked out of the house."[72]

As one of the men who participated in the CRB experience stated: "In HIV many things have been achieved, but when it comes to reducing stigma and discrimination, little progress has been made and even less on the subject if you are a woman . . . people do not think of her as a victim of HIV, but they relate to her as if she was a sex worker or as if she contracted it because she was looking for it."[73]

Tamar's story is repeated in several ways. In this participatory research guided by PAR, recourse to the CRB allowed the biblical text to illuminate and transform the reality of PLWHA. A careful and critical reading of the

70. Group 2, May 31, 2015.

71. Group 2, May 31, 2015.

72. Group 1. April 12, 2015.

73. Group 1. May 31, 2015.

narrative renewed the strength of those who fight for the rights of people who share their health status. This was the conclusion reached by the group of men who participated in this experience: "The situation that this woman lived through at that time is, at this moment, being experienced by people with the issue of HIV."[74]

The members of Huellas de Arte will continue to fight against the stigmatization and self-stigmatization of those who know their HIV-positive status. After having critically examined their own situation through a careful reading of this biblical text, they have new motivations to make sense of their thankless task. This is as important as it is difficult.

Final Observations

Gender-based violence is a violation of the fundamental rights associated with individual and community identities. Depending on the circumstances, anyone can be a victim of this type of violence, even men, but this scourge is closely associated with violence against women. It cuts across interpersonal relationships, social structures, and cultural matrixes. At these three levels, this violence limits women's sexual rights,[75] and this is a serious problem that cannot be ignored by theology.

Women often suffer direct sexual violence, but also structural violence from authorities, health care institutions, and Christian churches. In addition, they must endure the cultural violence of a patriarchal and sexist society. If they are women living with HIV, as is the case with the members of Huellas de Arte, they are also subject to discrimination because they have been infected with the HIV virus. Such discrimination also occurs at interpersonal, structural, and social levels.

The narrative of Tamar's rape and self-stigmatization was read through this reality. The experience of this CRB went beyond its initial scope, because having been victims of sexual violence themselves, these women shared their experiences beyond the restrictions established by their health condition. In the monthly meetings, they found a safe place to share the painful experiences that have affected their lives. In the conversation in the light of the biblical text, they became aware of their own capacity to transform the adverse social, economic, political, and cultural milieu in which they live.

---

74. Group 3. May 31, 2015.
75. Group 3. May 31, 2015. Galtung, "Violence, Peace, and Peace Research."

A careful reading of the text via various playful exercises, such as painting and dramatization, allowed Huellas de Arte participants to appropriate their reality critically and find appropriate means for its transformation. Beyond the realm of faith communities, this dialectic between the sacred text and life corresponds to the liberating role that churches must play in the contemporary secular world: "Valued in the light of their original context and also in the context of the present reader, the sources bring new meanings when challenged by the evangelical principle that seeks the liberating meaning of the mission of the Church."[76]

In addition to corroborating the need to overcome self-stigmatization as a first step to freeing oneself from discrimination and creating better living conditions for women, the CRB demonstrated the need to generate new masculinities, from which men can build their identity without violence against women. The development of new masculinities would not only prevent direct sexual violence but would also help to transform the social structures of discriminatory and sexist cultures.

A theology attentive to the transformations necessary to make the Kingdom of God a reality, which also favors the interpretation of the Holy Scriptures in the light of the reality that people live, is favored when it is generated in direct contact with those who suffer injustice. The struggle against the limitation of women's sexual rights and gender-based violence makes theological reflection relevant, by demonstrating its consistency with the prophetic message of the Gospel.

Although the Huellas de Arte Foundation began a new productive project with this Participatory Action Research (PAR), which others have now joined, perhaps the most important result was the mutual transformation achieved by the academics and members of the organization. The bonds of solidarity created in the shared struggle for recognition of the rights of women living with HIV/AIDS have made the liberating force of revelation evident when biblical texts pass through the lives of people and communities willing to be affected by them.

Reading the story of Tamar—the victim of David, Jonadab, Amnon, and Absalom—members of Huellas de Arte found new reasons and new strength to stand up for the sexual rights of women, especially those living with and coexisting with HIV. Now, they have begun reading another text on gender-based violence (Judges 19:1–30), to advocate for equity and justice, and continue developing their individual and collective capacities through CRB.

76. López, "Reading 2 Samuel 13:1–22," 13.

Bibliography

Andersson, Arnold. 2 Samuel. World Biblical Commentary 11. Waco: World, 1989.

Auld, A. Graeme. I and II Samuel: A Commentary. Lousville: Westminster John Knox Press, 2011.

Ávila, Catalina. "¿Qué está pasando con el Sida en Colombia?" UN Periódico 139 (2010) 17.

Boff, Clodovis. "Epistemología y método de la teología de la liberación." In Mysterium Liberationis. Conceptos fundamentales de la teología de la liberación, edited by Ignacio Ellacuría y Jon Sobrino, 79–113. San Salvador: UCA Editores, 1993.

Croatto, José. Hermenéutica práctica. Quito: Centro Bíblico Verbo Divino, 2002.

Dreher, Carlos. The Walk to Emmaus. São Leopoldo: CEBI, 2004.

Equipo de Docencia e Investigación Teológica. "Didaskalia. Fundación Huellas de Arte." Transcripciones de las grabaciones digitales de los encuentros. Bogotá, 2016.

Equipo de traductores de la edición española de la Biblia de Jerusalén. Biblia de Jerusalén. Bilbao: Desclée de Brower, 2009.

Fals, Orlando. "Action Research in the Convergence of Disciplines." International Journal of Action Research 9 (2013) 155–67.

———. "La ciencia y el pueblo: nuevas reflexiones." In La investigación-acción participativa. Inicios y desarrollos, edited by María Salazar, 65–84. Bogotá: Magisterio, 2013.

Fokkelman, Jan. Narrative Art and Poetry in the Books of Samuel. Vol. 1. King David. Assen: Van Gorcum, 1981.

Galtung, Johan. "Violence, Peace, and Peace Research." Journal of Peace Research 6 (1969) 167–91.

Khabure, Louise. "The Tamar Campaign Seminar. Breaking the Chain of Silence." In The Fellowship of Christian Councils and Churches in the Great Lakes and The Horn of Africa (FECCLAHA) edited by Nairobi, World Council of Churches (WCC), 2005.

López, Edgar. La evangelización como práctica interpretativa. Bogotá: Facultad de Teología. Pontificia Universidad Javeriana, 2009.

———. "Reading 2 Sam 13:1–22 from a Sexual Violence and HIV Perspective." In Mending the World? edited by Niclas Blåder and Kristina Helgesoon, 319–31. Eugene, OR: Wipf & Stock, 2017.

Mesters, Carlos. Flor sin defensa. Bogotá: Confederación Latinoamericana de Religiosos, 1987.

Ministerio de Salud y Protección Social. ONUSIDA. Plan Nacional de Respuesta ante las ITS-VIH/Sida 2014–2017. Bogotá, 2014.

Neuenfeldt, Elaine. "Sexual violence and power. The case of Tamar in 2 Samuel 13:1–22." Journal of Latin American Hermeneutics 3 (2007) 1–10.

Ricœur, Paul. Du texte à l' action. Essaisd' herméneutique II. Paris: Seuil, 1986.

Strauss, Anselm, and Juliet Corbin. Bases de la investigación cualitativa. Técnicas y procedimientos para desarrollar la teoría fundamentada. Medellín: Editorial Universidad de Antioquia, 2002.

West, Gerald. The Academy of the Poor: Towards a Dialogical Reading of the Bible. Sheffield: Sheffield Academic, 1999.

———. "The Contribution of Tamar's Story to the Construction of Alternative Masculinities." In Bodies, Embodiment, and Theology of the Hebrew Bible, edited by Tamar Kamionkowski and Kim Wonil, 184–200. London: T. & T. Clark, 2010.

West, Gerald, and Phumzile Zondi-Mazibela. "The Bible Story that Became a Campaign: The Tamar Campaign in South Africa (and Beyond)." *Ministerial Formation* 103 (2004) 4–12.

West, Gerald. "Do Two Walk Together? Walking with the Other Through Contextual Bible Study." *Anglican Theology Review* 93 (2011) 431–49.